ALL ABOUT

SPECIAL CD DEMONSTRATES 72 EFFECTS AND INCLUDES FULL SONG TRACKS!

EFFECTS

A FUN AND SIMPLE GUIDE TO UNDERSTANDING MUSIC EFFECTS

by MICHAEL ROSS

ISBN 978-1-4234-6845-5

T0057742

HAL•LEONARD®
CORPORATION

7777 W. BLUEMOUND RD. P.O. BOX 13819 MILWAUKEE, WI 53213

Copyright © 2010 by HAL LEONARD CORPORATION
International Copyright Secured   All Rights Reserved

For all works contained herein:
Unauthorized copying, arranging, adapting, recording, Internet posting, public performance,
or other distribution of the printed or recorded music in this publication is an infringement of copyright.

BRIEF CONTENTS

FULL CONTENTS

Page   CD Track

INTRODUCTION

ABOUT THIS BOOK

If you perform, record, or even just seriously listen to music, you need to know about effects. Whatever your relationship to music, *All About Effects* [AAE] is geared to serve as your introduction to the world of audio and MIDI processing. This book will help players of any instrument enlarge their palette of sounds, aid budding engineers in enhancing the music that they chronicle, and help fans — the consumers of recordings — understand more about what they are hearing.

All About Effects will tell you everything you need to know about common and some uncommon methods of shaping sound. It will cover all the effects in five basic categories:

- Equalization (active, passive, graphic, parametric, filtering)
- Distortion (fuzz, overdrive)
- Modulation (chorus, phasing, flanging, pitch shifting)
- Ambience (reverb, delay)
- Amplitude (volume pedals, tremolo, compression, gating)

We will also delve into some of the less common but equally evocative granular and spectral effects, used by sound designers and avant-garde musicians.

AAE will teach you tips and tricks of the pros, helping players and recordists decide which effects they need, and how to get more out of the effects they have. In addition, AAE will explain how these processors have been used in famous songs, and how you can use them creatively yourself. This book is unique in that it includes many audio examples to illustrate individual effects, as well as five full songs to demonstrate the use of effects in context.

What this book *won't* do is talk extensively about specific brand name effects. Many quality effects are widely available within each type, but to make this book as relevant twenty years from now as it is today, we will stick to the basic principles of each effect, without dwelling on a specific product unless it is essential to the understanding of that effect. Products come and go — principles stay the same.

We will also purposely *not* tell you which are the "best" sounds and effects. Effects are like condiments; mustard is not "better" than ketchup, and even within mustards, while some may have higher quality ingredients, you may prefer the taste of the cheap product to the gourmet brand. It is similar with effects. Some products may sound awful to one set of ears and beautiful to another. I hope that this book will help you develop your knowledge, ears, and sensitivity to the point where you can decide for yourself what sounds best to you.

What Do We Mean by Effects?

In the world of audio, effects are any process or device that affects the sound of the source signal, changing, among other things, its tone, amplitude (loudness), or the space in which it is perceived to exist.

Everyone is familiar with distorted rock guitar, but the sound doesn't start that way. Whether it is the singing, sustained sweetness of Eric Clapton's blues excursions or the buzz-saw rasp of Pantera's speed metal, the sound begins with undistorted, vibrating strings. It is only after they are processed through various effects pedals and/or a maxed-out guitar amplifier that these strings create the rainbow of overdrive, distortion, and fuzz that comprises the world of rock, fusion, and experimental guitar.

The drum kit used by Steve Gadd on hits by Michael McDonald did not vary greatly in terms of construction and basic sound from that played by Phil Collins on his early chart-toppers, yet Gadd's recorded drums sound natural, much like they might in a small room, while Collins created an instantly recognizable, thoroughly artificial sound using effects like compression and gating.

Finally, it is not just his soulful rasp that differentiates the records of Otis Redding from those of Cher and T-Pain, but the fact that the late legend's recorded vocals were electronically relatively unadorned, while the diva and the hip-hop artist make liberal use of an effect called auto-tune on their voices — not so much to correct their pitch, but as a way of creating an unusual sound.

Why Use Effects?

Every few years there seems to be a backlash against audio effects, with purists calling for a return to the "natural" sound of instruments and voices. Pure tone is indeed a thing of beauty, whether delivered by a lively old acoustic flattop guitar, a resonant concert grand piano, an orchestral quality violin, a warm, worn-in saxophone, an operatic soprano, or for that matter, a bowed saw. Even electronic musicians might prefer a character-laden, analog sine wave to a digital emulation.

Yet, in modern times, the experience of pure, unadulterated tone is rare. Unless you experience a sound directly from its source, in a non-reflective environment, you are not truly hearing "pure" tone. Once the sound is amplified through a PA system, recorded, or even heard acoustically in a reverberant symphony space, it is adulterated in some way — there is an "effect" of some sort on it.

You may think that in pre-electricity days it was more common to hear instruments and voices *au natural*, and you would be right; but even then, churches and concert halls were designed, in part, for the effect they would have on the music presented within their walls. Their echoing chambers lent an air of authority to the proceedings. It is even quite likely that early man went to the best sounding part of the cave to beat his rhythm stick — the first reverb.

Should you somehow be able to experience unfettered tone on a regular basis, you would find that it makes for a limited sonic palette. True, a great musician can produce a wide variety of sounds out of an unadorned instrument or voice, but that variety is still limited when compared to the infinite sonic possibilities created when you start adding effects. Properly employed, effects can add color and emotion to any sound, be it falling rain or a wailing rock singer.

Effects are used in recording and mixing to help us distinguish individual sounds from each other, while at the same time acting as a glue that pulls all the sounds together into a unified whole. The bottom line is that any sound you create or work with is most likely going to be artificially "effected" in some way, so you might as well learn how to control those effects — and have fun with them as well.

Do I Need to Read Music?

Not at all, though it always helps. You can certainly learn riffs and songs by ear from listening to the CD. Or, you can just listen to the CD to further your understanding of how the effects alter and enhance the sound.

What Equipment Do I Need?

If you bought this book, you most likely play an instrument — that's a start. Whether you do or don't, you are lucky; you live in a marvelous age. You can check out many of the effects discussed in this book being demonstrated on YouTube, or if you don't mind a small learning curve, by downloading one of the free or demo Digital Audio Workstations (DAWs) available online, and loading it with the dozens of free audio plug-ins also available on the internet. (Check out kvraudio.com for loads of free stuff).

You can just plug your instrument directly into your computer, or use your mouse to play one of the many free, downloadable synthesizers that have a virtual keyboard.

I highly recommend that you download the free Mac or PC demo of Ableton Live (ableton.com). If you don't have an instrument-to-computer interface, you can drag almost any audio sample directly into this easy-to-operate software. It comes with its own plug-in versions of most of the effects discussed in this book. You can drag them into a track and instantly hear the effect being discussed in the current chapter.

ABOUT THE CD

The CD included with this book offers audio examples of effects in use, clarifying the sounds that they produce and the many ways in which they can be used. Audio examples are paired with the audio icon to the left of the text; simply match the icon number to the CD track number.

COMMON TERMS USED IN THIS BOOK

Analog: a process that deals with the original waveform of the sound and the infinite number of points along that wave.

Attenuate or Attenuation: This refers to controlling the level of the volume or of an amount of an effect.

DAW: stands for Digital Audio Workstation, referring to recording systems like Pro Tools, Logic, Cubase, Digital Performer, and Ableton Live.

Digital: (as applies to sound) a waveform sampled at various points along the wave, converting those samples to ones and zeros.

Distortion: An alteration that takes place when an amplifier reaches the level at which it can no longer increase the output signal without altering the input signal.

Dry: This refers to an unaffected signal, heard as it sounds directly from the source.

Effects Loop: 1. A set of inputs and outputs that allow you to insert an effect or effects in between an amplifier's preamp and power amp sections, or the signal path within another effect. For example, the Electro-Harmonix Memory Boy lets you plug another effect into its effect loop. 2. A pedal that accepts other pedals into a set of ins and outs, letting you engage multiple effects with the switch of one button.

Expression Pedal: a treadle pedal similar to a wah or volume pedal that sends continuous controller signals through MIDI to control parameters of electronic devices like effects or synthesizer parameters.

Fader: A fader is a control that slides up and down along a track, as opposed to a knob that rotates.

Looping: This has nothing to do with an effects loop. It means taking a piece of audio and playing it back in such a way that when it reaches the end, it starts over.

MIDI (Musical Instrument Digital Interface): An industry-standard protocol that enables electronic musical instruments such as keyboard controllers, computers, and other electronic equipment to communicate, control, and synchronize with each other.

Native: Software powered by the CPU of the computer in which it is installed is called "native" software, as opposed to coming with additional hardware that takes the processing strain off of the host computer, like Pro Tools TDM or UAD effects.

Plug-in: a software device that inserts into a DAW's audio, MIDI, or aux tracks, and affects the sound being recorded or mixed.

Rack: Rack or Rack unit refers to an effect housing that can be mounted along with other rack units in a 19-inch rack. Rack units can be the full 19 inches wide, or can be half or third space units.

Unity Gain: This means that the volume of the signal coming out of the effect is the same as the volume going into the effect.

Wet: This refers to the application of an effect to a signal. It is sometimes used to label a control that adds the effect.

ICON LEGEND

Included in every *All About* book are several icons to help you on your way. Keep an eye out for these.

AUDIO
This icon indicates a related track on the accompanying CD.

NUTS & BOLTS
This icon highlights important explanations of fundamental concepts.

TRY THIS
Included with this icon are various suggestions for ways to expand your musical horizons.

EXTRAS
This includes additional information on various topics that may be interesting and useful, but not necessarily essential.

DON'T FORGET
There's a lot of information in this book that may be difficult to remember. This refresher will help you stay the course.

DANGER!
Here, you'll learn how to avoid injury and keep your equipment from going on the fritz.

ORIGINS
Interesting historical blurbs present for fun background information.

Volume

CHAPTER 1
VOLUME CONTROL

> **What's Ahead:**
> - Volume as an effect
> - Types of volume controls
> - Volume in recording

VOLUME AS AN EFFECT

Volume is more than something that club owners and old people tell you to turn down. Minute differences in the parameters of how quickly a sound reaches full volume, then fades and disappears, help us identify what instrument we are hearing.

- *Attack:* A distorted guitar and a cello have very similar sonic characteristics, but the picked guitar note reaches its loudness peak quicker than a bowed cello string, and this helps us discern the difference. The speed at which the sound reaches its highest level of volume is called the "attack," and being able to control this can greatly affect the character of an instrument's sound.

- *Decay:* "Decay" is another characteristic of sound. It refers to how quickly the note drops off from its full volume to its "sustain" volume.

- *Sustain:* "Sustain" is the volume at which the note lingers after its initial decay.

- *Release:* Finally, "release" is how quickly the sound fades after the source of its generation is removed: i.e., lifting your finger off of the guitar string, or key on a piano or synthesizer.

These factors can contribute to the sonic character of guitars, pianos, synthesizers, woodwinds, drums, and even vocals. We will be discussing each of these parameters many times over the course of this book. Taking control of these parameters lets you change the character of a sound source in interesting ways. In this section, we will focus on these parameters as they relate to the volume of a musical sound.

> The attack, decay, sustain, and release characteristics of a sound are referred to as its *envelope*, and those parameters are often shorthanded as ADSR.

TYPES OF VOLUME CONTROLS

There are many non-electronic ways to manipulate the character of these volume-based parameters. Pianos have a (misnamed) sustain pedal, which actually controls its release envelope while woodwind players use their tongues and airflow to adjust attack, decay, etc. String players modify their bowing technique, or switch to plucking the strings. Players of acoustic instruments, like drums, marimbas, pianos, and acoustic guitars have a certain amount of natural control over attack; playing harder or softer will affect it somewhat. They also have some command over the decay and sustain through touch, tuning, and damping. Synthesizers, electric guitar, and bass have greater ability to control these parameters. Guitarists and bassists can use the volume control on their instruments to swell notes, creating violin, cello, and even flute-style sounds.

On this track, you will hear the guitar emulating other instruments, using the volume control to manipulate the attack: first a cello and then a violin.

The way the volume reacts as you turn up a volume knob, rock a volume pedal forward, or slide a fader up is called the *taper*. Depending on the potentiometer (or "pot") used for the volume, you might experience a rapid gain when you first turn the control up from silence, and a slower gain further along the knob's rotation, or a slow gain initially and a big leap in the last quarter-turn. You should experiment with different pots to achieve the taper that works best for your application.

For violin and cello effects, a little overdrive helps simulate some of the overtones, similar to those present when a bow scrapes against strings. Depending on the way you create the distortion, this may work better if the distortion is before the volume control in the chain; try it both before and after to see which effect you prefer. For flute sounds, rolling back the tone control contributes to the mimicry. Adding reverb and/or delay can enhance the illusion as well.

Some musicians feel that having to manipulate the volume control on the instrument hampers their playing technique; one solution is a volume pedal.

Volume pedals have long been employed by pedal-steel players to help them get their trademark "crying" sound. Check out Tom Brumley's playing on the Buck Owens recording of the aptly named "Crying Time." These pedals are most often simply a volume potentiometer mounted in a pedal on the floor, operated by foot instead of hand. Many have a knob on the side that lets you set the minimum volume. This way you can set a rhythm level in heel position, then push the pedal to the toe position for lead. For effective emulation of other instruments, though, it is best to set the pedal so that it is off (or close to it) when in heel position.

Many volume pedals have an output for a tuner. This output continues to send a signal even when the volume is backed off so that no sound goes through the output of the pedal. This allows silent tuning.

One of the earliest volume effects on a pop record is George Harrison's attack-delayed notes on The Beatles' 1965 recording of "Yes It Is." The eerie effect produced brings an added element of melancholy to the already sad song.

There are effects available that swell the notes automatically, with no hand or foot manipulation necessary (other than turning on the pedal). Marketed as individual pedals, or as options in multi-effects, they have names like Attack Decay, Slow Gear, and Swell. They may have a sensitivity control and an attack control.

This device automatically slows the attack of the signal. The sensitivity (Sens) determines how hot the signal must be to be affected, while the Attack adjusts the length of time it takes for the signal to go from silence to full volume.

Most synthesizers have a full set of ADSR controls that let you fine-tune each aspect of a note's envelope. When you play a synthesizer with preset patches, you will notice that the lead patches have a quicker attack than the pads. By loading a file of a recorded acoustic or electric instrument into a sampler, you can modify its ADSR characteristics as if it were a synthesizer.

On this track, you will first hear some distorted guitar chords, then you will hear them played after being loaded into a sampler, with the sampler's ADSR controls modifying the sound by slowing the attack and shortening the decay.

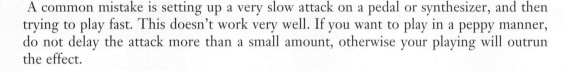

This virtual synthesizer has attack, decay, sustain, and release controls for both the volume of the oscillators and the envelope of the frequency controls.

Many hardware and software drum machines allow you to modify ADSR parameters for each drum. Hip-hop artists have created a new sound through the use of samplers. By slicing drum beats taken from vinyl records into their component parts (bass, snare, etc.), and controlling these parts from playable pads on the sampler, they are able to create new beats. The sampler also allows them change the envelope of each part of the beat, shortening the decay, or even reversing the sound so that the volume envelope of a drum hit swells up, rather than trailing off. Check out records by DJs Krush, Food, and Shadow to hear how they mangle essentially acoustic drum sounds into a world of fresh, rhythmic textures.

A common mistake is setting up a very slow attack on a pedal or synthesizer, and then trying to play fast. This doesn't work very well. If you want to play in a peppy manner, do not delay the attack more than a small amount, otherwise your playing will outrun the effect.

If you manipulate the instrument volume or foot pedal control very rapidly, you can emulate a tremolo effect (for a full explanation of tremolo, see the next section).

VOLUME IN RECORDING

Whatever instrument you play, if you record into a digital audio workstation (DAW) like Logic, Pro Tools, Cubase, or Ableton Live, you can create volume effects after you have committed the sound to a recorded track. Digital automation gives you full control over the envelope of any recorded sound. You can get interesting effects by drawing an automated volume swell into each note, as well as by playing with the decay.

One effect in the type of music known as "Glitch" involves cutting out sections of a recorded file, essentially dropping the volume to zero in those sections for a stuttering effect. This is actually an emulation of digital artifacts and dropouts, that rather than being considered flaws, are embraced as musical in this genre. Check out works by Telefon Tel-Aviv and Renfro for examples of how this technique can be used to create works of great beauty.

This acoustic drum loop is heard first in its natural state and then with the volume cut to zero on every other 1/256th note, creating a metallic glitch, effect. Then a guitar loop is added, first with no

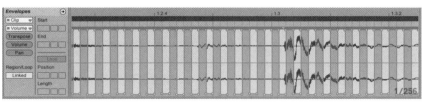

I have set the automation on this drum track to drop the volume to zero every other 1/256th of the beat.

volume effect, then with a glitchy rhythm created by introducing periodic 1/32nd notes of silence.

CHAPTER 2
TREMOLO

We introduced the term *tremolo* in the last chapter. In this one, you will learn exactly what it is and how to use it. You may be surprised to learn that this historic effect, associated with surf music, has many modern applications.

DEFINITION

Tremolo is essentially the controlled, rhythmic change of amplitude or volume. As described in the last chapter, rapidly moving either a volume knob or volume pedal emulates this effect, but to accurately create a tremolo rhythm, more mechanical methods are necessary. This is referred to as modulating the amplitude, hence, tremolo is often included in the modulation section of multi-effects. As amplitude, in this case, means volume, I chose to include it in the volume section of this book.

LFOS

In a modern tremolo effect, a low frequency oscillator, or LFO, modifies the amplitude. LFOs will appear frequently throughout the book, so it is best to have an understanding of how they work and what they do.

An oscillator is an electronically generated signal that, like a sound appearing in nature, travels in the form of a wave (see below), with the attendant peaks and valleys. How close together these waves appear is called the "frequency" and how high and low they go is called the "amplitude."

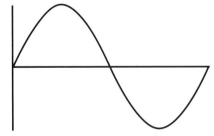

This is a simple sine wave. The peaks and the valleys represent the amplitude, while the distance from peak to peak is the frequency.

A low frequency oscillator usually puts out a frequency below 20 Hz, but its sound is not meant to be heard (see Understanding Frequencies in Chapter 8). Rather than being sent to an audio output, an oscillator is used only to modify another signal. In the case of tremolo, it is the volume of the original signal being affected by the tremolo. The frequency of the LFO is adjustable, and depending on whether it is higher or lower, the rate of the tremolo will be faster or slower. The amplitude of the LFO determines the depth of the effect.

Tremolo comes from the desire to emulate the practice, on acoustic instruments, of rapidly repeating one or two notes (sometimes called a trill). One of the first attempts to emulate this sound was on an electronic organ.

Much confusion has arisen over the years due to misuse of the terms tremolo and vibrato. Technically, tremolo refers to volume modulation, and vibrato refers to pitch modulation. Whammy bars on guitars have been called tremolo arms, but as they modify the pitch, they are more correctly called vibrato arms. Conversely, Fender amps often labeled the tremolo section "vibrato," when in fact, it only modulated the volume.

TYPES OF TREMOLO

For such a basic concept, the raising and lowering of volume, tremolo comes in many flavors. There is the tremolo that comes as part of vintage guitar amplifiers and electric pianos; tremolo effects that are available in pedals and plug-ins; tremolo effects created in synthesizers; and tremolo effects that can be created by waveform manipulation in digital recording software.

Guitar Amplifier Tremolo

Ever since the early days of guitar amplifiers, there have been models equipped with the tremolo effect. Early Fender, Ampeg, Danelectro, Gibson, and Vox amps used "bias modulation tremolo," where the volume fluctuation is achieved by manipulating the amp's power tube grid bias. This is still used in Vox and Ampeg amps but Fender later switched to an "opto" tremolo. This system employs a pulsing light source shining on a photo resistor to create the modulation. Opto tremolo tends to be smoother sounding than the choppier bias variety. In both cases an LFO controls the rate and the depth.

Tremolo is strongly associated with "Swamp Rock," one of the primary examples of which is Creedence Clearwater's "Born On the Bayou," and surf music, like the rhythm guitar on the Ventures' "Pipeline."

The first tremolo pedal was the DeArmond in the late 1940s–around the same time that Gibson also began putting the effect in their amps. The first Fender Amp with tremolo appeared in 1955. It was the aptly (and correctly) named Tremolux.

Tremolo Pedals

The tremolo effect, so popular in the 1950s and early 60s, fell out of favor in the late 60s. By the 70s, it was no longer offered in many amps. Though the concept had been around for decades, and Boss produced a pedal in the early 90s, tremolo didn't regain popularity until near the end of the millennium, when Alt-Country and "roots" music began to surge.

Today there are dozens of these effects produced by large manufacturers, as well as boutique pedal makers like Demeter, Fulltone, Cusack, Diamond, etc. The vast majority of these use the optical modulation method. These days, digital multi-effects, whether the rack-mounted or pedalboard style, also include tremolo in the modulation section.

Slicers

A "slicer" effect, whether in a multi-effects unit or a dedicated pedal like the Boss SL-20, is essentially a radical tremolo. The volume cut tends to be more extreme than with tremolo. You will find that the line is blurred these days by some boutique tremolos that offer settings approaching slicer-style effects. This effect can emulate the glitch effect used in recording.

This Slicer pedal produces glitch-style effects in a variety of rhythmic patterns.

On this track, you will hear the guitar run through a near-slicer-style tremolo created by the SoundToys Tremolator, a plug-in that allows it to synchronize perfectly with the drum groove.

Auto-Panning

Auto-Panning is a stereo effect that rhythmically moves the signal back and forth between the left and right side of the stereo spectrum. It is related to tremolo in that it raises and lowers the volume of the right and left channels to create the illusion that the sound is moving across the stereo field. If you were to convert an auto-panning effect to mono, you would have a tremolo effect.

This tremolo pedal offers stereo outputs for panning effects.

Software

If you are using digital recording software, there are a number of plug-ins that will create tremolo effects. Some let you tap the tempo in to match the groove of the song, but even better, many will automatically synchronize to the master tempo of the song, letting you lock into the groove.

This plug-in allows you to synchronize to the track tempo to add swing, shuffle, and accents to the tremolo rhythm.

TREMOLO CONTROLS AND WHAT THEY DO

The two basic tremolo controls are "rate" or "speed," and "depth," sometimes called "intensity."

- Rate adjusts how fast these changes take place, thus determining the rhythm.
- Depth determines the amount of variation between the loudest and softest volumes.

Modern tremolo pedals often include a tap-tempo option that allows you to synchronize the timing of the tremolo's rhythm with the tempo of the song. Some tremolo effects let you choose (or even create) rhythmic patterns other than straight eighth notes, quarter notes, etc.

Tremolos like the Cusack Tap-A-Whirl and the SoundToys Tremolator plug-in offer controls for ramp effects. This is when the tremolo rate increases or decreases automatically as the signal driving it fades away.

On this track, you will hear the tremolo rate slow down as the guitar chord fades away. For some added fun, I depressed the vibrato arm of the guitar so that the pitch falls away to create a sound like a motor winding down.

WAVEFORMS

Some tremolo pedals offer controls that let you choose a number of different waveforms for the LFO to create everything from vintage Fender-style tremolo to a randomly pulsing effect.

This is a good place to introduce the concept of *waveforms*, a term we will be mentioning throughout this book. Without getting too technical, sound travels through the air in a manner that resembles a wave on the ocean, with similar peaks and valleys. The most common waveforms are: Sine, Triangle, Sawtooth, and Square.

- A Sine wave suggests gently rolling seas with rounded off edges. A Fender-type, optical tremolo produces a sine wave, maintaining softness even at extremely intense settings.
- A Triangle wave looks like a row of pyramids placed end to end; its sharper peaks and troughs create a choppier sound, more like a bias tremolo.
- A Sawtooth wave is like a tsunami that rises up slowly, then falls off sharply (it can also be inverted — rising quickly, then falling off slowly). Sawtooth tremolos are dramatically rhythmic.
- A Square wave looks like a bunch of skyscrapers with flat spaces in between. This makes for a very choppy sound, associated with slicers.
- A Pulse wave is like a Square wave, but not as symmetrical.

        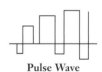

| Sine Wave | Triangle Wave | Sawtooth Wave | Square Wave | Pulse Wave |

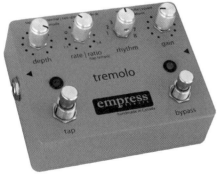

Some tremolos allow you to choose from a number of different waveforms, while others have a knob that goes gradually from one to another, offering variations on the basic form.

This tremolo pedal offers tap tempo and a variety of waveform options.

Run the signal from a hard chopping tremolo or slicer effect into a slow sweeping modulation effect like a filter, phaser, or flanger to break up the monotony of the repeating rhythmic pattern.

CHAPTER 3
COMPRESSION

What's Ahead:

- What is it?
- Understanding the basic compression parameters
- How does compression differ from limiting?
- Sidechaining
- Uses for bass, drums, guitar, vocals, and mixing and mastering

---

Compression is one of the most commonly used, yet least understood of the audio effects. While not all musicians use it in a live situation, many will have it applied by house sound engineers, and virtually all will encounter it in recording, where it may be applied while tracking, mixing, or mastering — often at all three stages. Yet most musicians, and a surprising number of engineers, are vague about how it works. You may not be an expert when you finish this section — that will only come with constant experimentation with the effect — but you will have a clearer picture of how this important effect molds your sound.

WHAT IS IT?

A compressor is essentially an automatic volume control. Its purpose is to ride herd on the gain level of whatever sound source is put through it. It can be used to make loud signals softer and soft signals louder. You could do this by continuously adjusting a volume pedal, or a fader on a mixing board, and in some cases, that is exactly what happens. But to control popping bass notes that break up speakers, loud snare hits that distort tape, or soft ones that get lost in the mix, you need a machine that can respond faster than a human.

A basic compressor is made up of a variable gain amplifier, a level detector, and a makeup gain amplifier. The level detector, as you might imagine, detects the level of the input signal and tells the variable gain amplifier whether to decrease it or not–depending on the compressor's parameter settings. The makeup gain amplifier allows you to once again match the input volume level after applying the effect.

This effect deals with *dynamic range*. The dynamic range of an instrument, or a recorded piece of music, is the difference between the softest and loudest audible notes. A compressor reduces the level of volume peaks, allowing the overall signal level to be turned up without damaging speakers, ears, or distorting recording gear. This gives the signal a higher average level, resulting in music that sounds louder and punchier than an uncompressed signal. The operative word is "sounds." By bringing the soft sounds closer in volume to the loud sounds, the music appears to be louder, even though the loudest parts are no louder than before.

This is called *reducing the dynamic range*, and is a topic of hot debate among recording, mixing, and mastering engineers. Some feel limiting the range from soft to loud loses the expressiveness of the music. Others feel that making the track sound louder is necessary to compete in the world of pop music.

Producers of early vinyl records found that if the signal got too loud, the needle would jump out of the groove. Compression was used to prevent any peaks from causing this to happen. This became less of a concern with the rise of CDs and MP3s, but given the renewed interest in pressing vinyl, this is good to know.

Instrumentalists sometimes use compressors to even out the level of the notes as they play, and/or add apparent sustain to those notes. Once again, the sustain is "apparent" rather than actual because the note itself is not lasting any longer than if it were not compressed; it is just that as the sound dies, the amplifier in the compressor keeps raising the volume back up, slowing the decay, and making it appear to last longer.

Strike a note on a guitar or bass and time the number of seconds until the note is completely gone. Then strike the same note with a compressor effect on it and time it again. You will find that the note is gone in the same amount of time, it just sounds louder longer.

UNDERSTANDING THE BASIC COMPRESSION PARAMETERS

Compressors can have anywhere from one knob to over a dozen controls. Nearly all compressors will have a knob marked output, gain, volume, or level. In more complex units, this might be called makeup gain, which is a good way to describe what it does. When you use a compressor to tamp down the volume peaks, it initially lowers the overall volume. The makeup gain control helps you "make up" the difference, bringing the volume back up to pre-compressed levels (or above).

Stompbox compressors usually have only two or three parameter controls. One will be the volume and the other knob might be marked sustain, sensitivity, or compression. The sustain control usually combines a number of different parameters that are more directly accessible in more complex units. Some pedals include a tone control, as inexpensive compressors are less than transparent, accentuating certain frequencies that you may not want. A few pedals include an attack control; this parameter is described below.

This famous "red box" compressor has only two controls, but has appeared on countless classics and hits.

A key to understanding compression is learning how the basic controls of a high-end compressor work. Here are some of the main parameters that need to be adjusted:

- Threshold: Threshold sets the input volume level at which the compression effect kicks in. Sounds below the threshold volume pass through unaltered. Only sounds above the threshold are compressed.

- Ratio: Signals above the threshold are attenuated by an amount specified by the Ratio parameter. For example, with a compression ratio of 4 (or 4:1), if a signal above the threshold increases by 4 dB (decibels), the compressor output will increase by only 1 dB. If a signal above the threshold increases by 8 dB, then the output will increase by only 2 dB.

- Knee: The knee control adjusts how gradually or abruptly compression occurs as the threshold is approached. With a setting of 0 dB, signals below the threshold will have no compression applied, and full compression is applied to any signal at or above the threshold. This is called *hard knee* behavior and can sound harsh with very high compression ratios. With higher (or softer) knee values, the compressor begins compressing gradually as the threshold is approached.

- Gain Reduction: Compressors often have a Gain Reduction meter, showing how much the gain is being reduced at any given moment. The more reduction, the more audible the effect.

- Attack and Release: These control the response time of the compression, in other words, how fast it reacts to input-level changes. Attack determines how quickly maximum compression is reached after a signal exceeds the threshold. Release tells the compressor how long to take before returning to normal operation once the signal has fallen below the threshold. A longer attack time allows peaks to come through unprocessed, helping to preserve some dynamics. Extremely short release times can cause a pumping or sucking effect. This is usually an undesirable effect, but some producers use it as a rhythmic enhancement on drum tracks.

This studio compressor mounts in a rack and offers a multitude of controls, as well as gain reduction meters.

You would think that a compressor could only react to an input signal once it occurs, and might be late in applying these attack and release envelopes. Digital compressors, however, can solve the problem by delaying the input signal; this is called "look-ahead compression."

Compressors can have differing characteristics:

- Peak: Peak compressors react to short peaks within a signal.
- RMS: RMS-type units are less sensitive to short peaks, compressing only when the level exceeds the threshold for a slightly longer time; they deal with more of an average level.

- Optical: Due to the physics of turning electricity to light and back again, optical compressors exhibit a non-linear release curve; that is, the release is initially fast, then slows as the gain reduction approaches zero.

Each type has its uses: Peak compressors work to ensure that there are absolutely no signals over the set threshold. RMS is considered a bit more musical, while optical compressors are smooth and natural sounding, often used on vocals, bass, and electric guitar. Compressors can also come in feedforward and feedback versions. Feedforward models analyze the loudness of the incoming signal while a feedback compressor analyzes the output of the device and then self-adjusts its compression behavior. The attack and release parameters of feedback compressors are a bit less precise, but feedback compression generally results in a much smoother sound, offering less overall gain reduction, but less potential for distortion.

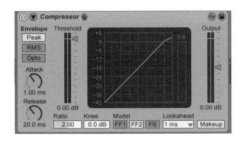

This compression plug-in from Ableton Live features peak, RMS, and optical compression options, as well as Feedforward and Feedback modes.

When tubes are used in guitar, bass, and recording amplifiers, or outboard effects like EQ, this can also cause compression. This also adds a type of distortion that music lovers have come to find pleasing. These characteristics are present in tube-driven compressors, causing them to be highly prized.

On this track you will hear a funk-rhythm guitar part, first uncompressed and then highly compressed.

HOW DOES COMPRESSION DIFFER FROM LIMITING?

A limiter's job is to ensure that the output does not exceed a specified level. Limiters are often used on the master output of a mixer to prevent clipping (an unpleasant form of distortion).

A limiter is essentially a compressor with a 10:1 or higher ratio, a fast attack time, and a relatively high threshold. The idea is not to squash the dynamics but to prevent any peaks that might distort the amplifier, mixing board, tape, DAW, or speakers from getting through. Almost any high-end compressor can act as a limiter. Brick-wall limiting has a very high ratio, 20:1 all the way up to ∞ (infinity):1, and a very fast attack time to ensure that an audio signal never exceeds the amplitude of the threshold.

SIDECHAINING

There are occasions when you may want to compress a signal, but only at certain moments. For example, you find that a punchy bass line is covering up the bass drum part, but you don't want to change the sound of either, you just want the bass to come down when the bass drum hits; or, having made the vocals bright enough to cut through a complex mix, you find that when the singer sings words containing the letter "S," they are now painfully sibilant. This is where a process called *sidechaining* comes in.

Many studio compressors have an input that can send a second signal source to the effect's level detector. This is called a sidechain, and allows the amount and timing of the compression to be controlled by a signal other than the one being processed.

For example, by splitting off the bass drum signal and sending it to the sidechain of a compressor that is affecting the bass, you can insure that the bass level drops a bit each time the bass drum is hit.

Our sibilant vocal issue is a little different. In this case, the vocal is split into two parts. One is sent to the main input of a compressor and the other is sent to the sidechain input. We don't want to merely increase the compression of the vocal, but rather only increase it on the more sibilant parts. To do this, an EQ is placed on the vocal signal that is sent to the sidechain input to boost the frequencies where the "S" sound and other sibilants reside, while de-emphasizing the other frequencies. This way the compressor will only kick in when the vocal gets sibilant. A compressor used this way is often called a "de-esser."

At the start of this track you will hear a drum track with the bass drum on every beat (or quarter note) and an eighth-note synth-bass track with two notes on every beat. Next you will hear the bass sidechain compressed by the bass drum. Now the bass is squashed when the bass drum plays and released in the spaces, allowing the bass drum to be more prominent. (For demonstration purposes, the effect is more extreme than the amount you would normally apply.)

Multi-band compression offers another way of controlling specific frequencies. A multi-band compressor allows you to apply compression only to a specific EQ range. This will be thoroughly covered in the section on spectral effects.

USES OF COMPRESSION FOR BASS, DRUMS, GUITAR, VOCALS, MIXING, AND MASTERING

Compression may be used on all instruments and in all stages of the recording process. It is a very flexible and often subtle effect. The best way to learn how to use it is to practice like you would with an instrument. Here are some tips for applying it in different situations.

- Bass: Whether acoustic or electric, playing jazz, rock, or funk, uncontrolled bass can really muddy up a mix. A quick attack can tighten up some sloppy playing. For slapping and popping, you may want a slower attack to let the excitement of the style shine through, but keep a close eye on the threshold to prevent distortion. Tentatively played bass notes can easily get lost in the mix whether live or in recording; let your ears tell you what ratio strikes the best balance between audibility and dynamics.

- Drums: Applied to the whole kit, where all the mics have been routed to a stereo mix, compression can glue the groove together, as well as make the drums sound bigger. Used on individual drums, it can even out the level of the kick, fatten the snare, or rein in an errant crash cymbal. The usual rule of thumb is if you can actually hear the compression, it is too much. Occasionally though, producers and/or engineers will want to push the compression to where there is an audible breathing or pumping effect evident as a part of the rhythm.

- Guitar: Compression has many uses with guitar in both live and recording situations. High-ratio, low-threshold squashing makes funk rhythms pop out of a track, while long release times can increase apparent sustain, enhancing volume swells and modulation effects like mild pitch shifting and chorus. Adrian Belew's rhythm guitar on the King Crimson tune, "Elephant Talk" (on the *Discipline* record), is heavily compressed by an MXR Dynacomp pedal, making it leap out at you. His compression remains on at all times, adding sustain to overdriven solos as well. Mild compression can make all the notes of a strummed acoustic guitar ring equally, as well as taming bass boom, midrange squawk, and high-end shriek; just be careful as it can also boost finger noise. The acoustic guitar at the beginning of Sarah McLachlan's "Building a Mystery" is tastefully compressed, letting all the notes come through equally, while taming any boom on the low end.

- Vocals: Ideally, singers know proper microphone technique, backing away for loud notes and moving up close for the softer ones, thus maintaining a consistent, undistorted vocal level. For those whose technique is suspect, a compressor can keep those dangerously loud notes under control and bring up intimate whispers to where they can be heard above raucous drums or guitars. Singers with good technique may be using a microphone with what is known as a proximity effect. This means that the tone changes depending on the distance from the mic. In that case, a compressor can ride levels while the singer maintains a constant distance from the microphone. With headset mics, compression is a must.

- Mixing: As mentioned, compression can be crucial in helping sonic details emerge from a crowded mix. You may find yourself wanting to use it on almost every track. That is why it is important to use as little as possible during the recording process, as you will be adding more during the mix (and still more in mastering). A little compression at each stage is better than a lot at once. Compressing the whole mix a little at the master output can make the mix sound more "finished," like a master recording. This can help you make decisions about individual amounts of compression. It is usually best, however, to remove this compression before sending the mix to be mastered, which brings us to…

- Mastering: This where the final mix is magically turned into a professional-sounding recording. Among other things, a mastering engineer will apply compression, often multi-band, in an effort to bind the whole sound together, making each individual track sound like part of the whole. If you are going for the loudest mix possible, it is important that you do a good deal of your compression on the individual tracks; if you try to achieve this loudness by just compressing or limiting the whole mix in mastering, you risk radically changing the balance of your mix.

Compression is a useful effect to help instruments cut through in a live situation or a mix, as well as providing glue that can bind a recorded mix together. Be aware that it can be very difficult to hear its effect until it is applied extremely, so be careful that you don't overdo it and suck the dynamic life out of your playing or a mix.

CHAPTER 4

EXPANSION AND GATING

What's Ahead

- Expansion vs. Compression
- Parameters
- Uses for expansion
- Gating
- Uses for gating

EXPANSION VS. COMPRESSION

Perhaps as a kid you played "opposite" day, where everything meant the opposite of what you said; or maybe you are a Superman fan and familiar with the concept of Bizarro World, where everything was the opposite of the way it was on earth. An *expander* is sort of a "Bizarro" compressor. Its construction is virtually the same: a variable gain amplifier, a level detector, and a makeup gain amplifier. The level detector still detects the level of the input signal, but rather than lowering the level when the input signal gets above the threshold, an expander lowers the level further when the input signal goes below its threshold. An expander can also be considered an automatic volume control; it is the equivalent of pulling a fader down once the input signal goes below a certain volume.

Expanders are often used to reduce noise in recording. Normally, as the signal from an instrument or voice dies out, any background noise becomes more audible. An expander's level detector takes note of the disappearing input signal, and when it gets below a certain point, pulls the level down so that the background noise is less prominent. It then brings the level back up when the instrument or voice begins again.

There are two types of expanders: upward and downward, but the upward variety is very rare. It increases the level when the input signal is above the threshold. This runs a risk of distortion and must be used very carefully. What is commonly called an expander is almost always a downward expander.

PARAMETERS

An expander has many of the same parameters as a compressor, but like the threshold, they tend to work in a reverse manner.

- Slope: An expander's "slope" parameter is equivalent to a compressor's ratio. It determines how much the signal is attenuated once it drops below the threshold. For example, a 1:2 slope means that a signal that enters the expander at 10 dB below the threshold will leave at 20 dB below. Unlike a compressor's ratio, an expander's slope is rarely adjustable, more often being fixed within the hardware or the software's programming.
- Attack: While the attack parameter on a compressor determines how quickly the signal is attenuated once it rises above the threshold, an expander's attack function sets how fast the signal is un-attenuated once it rises above the threshold.

- Release: Sometimes called fade or decay, this is the setting that determines how quickly the level is brought down once the signal goes below the threshold.
- Hold: Expanders have some controls not present on compressors. Sometimes when a singer holds a note, or a guitar chord decays, the level will drop below the threshold before the music dies away completely. If the expander were to lower the level as soon as the signal was below the threshold, it would sound unnatural. The hold parameter allows the note to continue for a second or more after going below the threshold to fall away more naturally.
- Range: To create an even more natural effect, the range control lets you restrict how much the expander can diminish the signal. If you prefer, rather than going all the way down to silence, you can set a specific minimum level. Sometimes, leaving a little noise between the notes makes for a more realistic recording.

USES FOR EXPANSION

Downward expansion is used primarily to reduce the volume level of unwanted audio in the spaces between the desired sounds. This can include hiss from tape or hardware, hum from amplifiers or guitar pickups, outside noises intruding on poorly soundproofed rooms or studios, and the like. It can also be used to tame leakage into adjacent microphones, for example, a snare drum leaking into a tom microphone. By placing an expander across a tom track and setting the threshold above the level of the snare and high-hat leakage, you can greatly reduce the amount of snare and hat picked up by the tom mic.

Expansion can also be *sidechained* (sometimes called keyed), whereby the level of the signal that it is attenuated is controlled by a second signal sent to the level detector. This can be used for an effect called *ducking*. Ducking is used in broadcasting or advertising to ensure that background music gets softer when the announcer is speaking, returning to its normal level as soon as the talking ceases. Though this could be done with compression, the rising and falling of natural speech might cause the music to fluctuate in level. The range function of an expander ensures that the music will stay at a consistent volume when the announcer is speaking by pushing its level down against the minimum allowed reduction.

Ducking is sometimes used with delay effects to keep the repeats from obscuring the original signal. An expander reduces the delay volume while the original signal is present, bringing it up when the input signal stops, and allowing the repeats to trail off.

GATING

Gating relates to expanding much the way limiting relates to compression: it is largely a matter of degree. While expansion somewhat diminishes unwanted audio, gating usually refers to extreme reduction, almost or all the way to silence. Gating requires fine-tuning of the attack, release, hold, and range parameters, otherwise unwanted noise can stutter into occasional audibility.

USES FOR GATING

Sometimes you may want absolutely no leakage between the drums in a kit; radical gating can help with this. If a bass part is not locked in with the bass drum, you can sidechain a gate on the bass to let it through only when the bass drum hits, or you might have a high-gain guitar part that needs to start and stop with no other instruments playing, and you want to mask its unwanted noise. A gate can eliminate pickup or amp hum in the spaces by setting the threshold above the level of the noise, but below the level of the guitar parts.

As you can see, these situations are similar to those in which you would use expansion. The difference is partly an artistic decision: you either think a little bit of noise and/or leakage adds to the overall sound or you don't. This can change on a case-by-case basis, depending on the music.

Gating can also be used to create new musical sounds. By sidechaining or "keying" a gate to open a continually playing low synthesizer note whenever the bass drum hits, you can create a bass part or a tuned bass drum sound. Keying a gate on the guitar part off of the hi-hat achieves a slicing tremolo sound.

The most famous gating effect is when a large room reverb (either natural or artificial) is compressed to increase the length of the decay, then cut short by a gate. This creates a sound not heard in nature, sometimes called the Phil Collins or Peter Gabriel effect. This effect is often keyed to the snare to keep the drums from getting muddy.

This noise gate pedal can remove single-coil hum or hiss from a high gain amp setting as long as no notes are being played.

"Noise gate" often refers to the rack units and pedals used by guitarists. These are essentially downward expanders that cut off the noise caused by high-gain amps and buzzing pickups when the guitarist stops playing. The pedals should be used judiciously, as they have fewer controls than a professional gate and can cut off sustain if set too high.

First you will hear a snare drum run through a reverb set to "large chamber," with a compressor increasing the level of the reverb's decay. Then you will hear a gate added to artificially cut off the decay, making for a fat, but concise snare sound.

CHAPTER 5
TRUE BYPASS AND BUFFERING

> ***What's Ahead***
> * What is true bypass?
> * What is buffering?
> * Buffer pedals
> * Loops and switching systems

WHAT IS TRUE BYPASS?

The controversy over *true bypass* switching in pedal effects rages through the stompbox community. True bypass means that when a pedal is off, the signal goes from the input jack directly to the output jack without going through any components (resistors, capacitors, op amps, etc.) on the circuit board. Without true bypass, when pedals are turned off there may be high-end loss from the signal bleeding into the components.

Many effects, like MXR pedals, most Electro-Harmonix pedals, many wahs, and most pedals from before 1980 use a Single-Pole Double Throw (SPDT) switch. This type of switch has only three terminals. With SPDT switches, when the effect is off, the guitar signal goes directly to the output jack but is still connected to the input of the effect's circuitry, and some high end is lost this way. The more expensive six terminal Double-Pole Double Throw (DPDT) switches allow the signal to bypass the input of the circuitry when in the off position.

While true bypass insures that individual pedals do not reduce your signal's integrity, combining a bunch of them with the cable joining them, as well as the cable to and from the pedalboard, can still result in significant signal loss, due to the capacitance of the cables themselves. Also, true bypass pedals can sometimes cause a loud "pop" when first engaged. This is because the input and output capacitors on the effect leak current. When bypassed in a true bypass circuit the capacitors are open circuited. While open, current leakage shifts their DC voltage, so that, when the effect is once again engaged, these capacitors must charge back to their normal voltage. The sudden voltage difference and charging current is heard in the amplifier as a pop. If the effect has any gain, say in an overdrive or distortion pedal, the pop is further amplified. The problems of cable capacitance and current leakage can be solved by something called buffering.

WHAT IS BUFFERING?

A *buffer* is a small amplifier used to maintain signal level through the long trip from instrument to amp or mixing board. Even a player who plugs directly into a combo, without using any pedals, can suffer signal loss if a long (20 feet or more) or cheap cable is used to make the connection. Ideally a buffer amp should provide a small, totally transparent boost to the signal in order to maintain what is called *unity gain*.

Unity gain is the state in which the volume at the input of a device is equal to the volume at the output of the device. Many devices and effects have either preset or controllable amplifiers as part of their circuitry to make sure that the gain going in equals the gain coming out.

Many modern pedals (Boss and Ibanez) use electronic switching and contain buffers. This prevents capacitance pops and volume loss due to cable length, but should you use a number of these pedals, the multiplication of their less-than-top-quality buffers will overly color and possibly degrade the signal.

The optimum solution would be to use as many true bypass pedals as possible in combination with one or two effects that contain buffered switching, or a dedicated buffer built into a custom pedal board. This type of buffer is not usually adjustable and is set by the designer of the pedalboard to offer just the right boost to maintain signal integrity. There may be one or more of these depending on the amount and types of pedals involved.

BUFFER PEDALS

A buffer pedal is not like a boost pedal in that it makes no attempt to create distortion (anything but); nevertheless, a boost pedal can be used as a buffer. Any clean boost pedal (like the Xotic RC Booster, the Durham Sex Drive, the MXR Custom Audio Electronics MC-401 Boost Line Driver, or dozens of others) that is left on all the time will help reduce signal loss from multiple pedals and/or long cables. Just keep the level low enough to avoid distorting your clean tones.

Do not put a buffer or boost pedal between your guitar and a vintage fuzz like a Fuzz Face, a modern facsimile, or other germanium effects like treble booster/rangemaster style pedals. A Fuzz Face interacts directly with guitar pickups so that it will clean up when the instrument volume is rolled down. The pickup and volume knobs actually become part of the fuzz circuit. A buffer or buffered pedal before the germanium pedals will cause you to lose the interaction with the Fuzz Face and other germanium pedals, and will cause the fuzz to get unmusically bright sounding. Put these pedals in the effects chain first–before any buffers or buffered pedals.

LOOPS AND SWITCHING SYSTEMS

Another way around the signal degradation problem is to place effects into a switchable, buffered loop. The effects loop on the back of an amplifier works this way, using the preamp of the amplifier to buffer the signal.

Be careful with amplifier effects loops. Some put out levels that are too much for stompbox pedals and should only be used with effects that accept the higher "line" level. Check with the manufacturer of both amp and pedal to see if they are compatible.

Companies like Radial Engineering sell individual loop pedals that will remove tone altering effects whether buffered or not, from the signal path. These loop pedals offer high-quality buffering to maintain an accurate signal when the pedal in the loop is bypassed. Some can also adjust for volume differences when the effects pedal is engaged.

For those with a multitude of pedals, as well as rack effects, it is often best to use a full-on, buffered, MIDI switching system. Whether custom-built by gear gurus Bob Bradshaw or Pete Cornish, or put together on your own using switchers by Voodoo Labs or Carl Martin, these systems usually allow every effect to be placed in or out of the signal path at will, as well as offering buffering options, and the ability to turn a number of effects on and off at will.

Plug your instrument directly into the amp using a relatively short cable, then play and listen. Now plug it into one effect before plugging the effect into the amp, using a very short cable to minimize signal loss due to cable length. Listen again with the effect off. This should give you an idea of what you are losing when running through this effect. Remember this loss is cumulative, increasing with each effect and extra length of cable.

SECTION **2**

Equalization

CHAPTER 6
FREQUENCIES

What's Ahead:

- Understanding frequencies
- Frequencies of specific sounds

UNDERSTANDING FREQUENCIES

As a user of tone controls on stereos, instrument amplifiers, and such, you are already familiar with basic tonal ranges like bass and treble. You already know that treble deals with the bright end of the sound spectrum, while bass is the lower, rumbling portion of the sound. More sophisticated tone-shaping involves both a wider range of tones and a narrower focus on each section of this range.

Tones are most often broadly separated into bass, mid-range and high-end; sometimes high mid-range and low mid-range will be added to the general description. Serious manipulation of tone requires defining its range in many specific frequencies.

A tone's frequency is described in terms of *hertz* (Hz). Hertz is defined as the number of cycles per second. When used to talk about sound, it refers to sound wave vibration. These vibrations translate into both pitch and tone, and can be very confusing, but for our purposes, hertz will be an indicator of the tonal range.

The human ear can hear tones ranging from roughly 20 hertz to 20 kilohertz. A kilohertz (kHz or sometimes just K) is 1000 hertz, so we can technically hear up to 20,000 hertz–at least some younger people still can. Age and exposure to loud music can significantly reduce the ability to hear, so turn down those ear buds!

The lower hertz numbers refer to bass tones, while the higher numbers represent treble tones. As you can imagine, with 18,080 hertz to choose from, we can greatly fine-tune a particular sound, or group of sounds, like a recorded mix.

origins

The term equalization comes from the early days of electronic audio (the 19th century), when the audio signal put into a device was greatly degraded in sound quality when it came out. An equalizer's job was to make the tone of the output signal more equal to that of the input.

FREQUENCIES OF SPECIFIC SOUNDS

Instruments get elements of their personality from certain frequencies. Here is a rough guide to the various ranges.

Sub-Bass

(20hz-40hz)

This range is below most instruments except the lowest pedal notes of a pipe organ and some sub-bass generators on synthesizers. Sounds in this range are restricted to either effects in movies with surround-sound systems (like thunder or earthquakes), or bass and bass drum tones for dance clubs. Sounds down here are felt as much as heard.

Bass

(40hz-80hz)
This is where music's bottom end lives in the bass drum, bass fiddle, or electric bass guitar, and also includes any low-end piano or synthesizer bass.

(80hz-100hz)
While boosting this frequency can add heft to a thin sound, it is also where any boominess lies. The upper end of a bass fundamental and the lower end of a guitar overlap here. Floor toms, and the lower reaches of pianos, organs and some voices can also be found in this range.

Bass/Lower Mid-Range

(200Hz-600Hz)
This is the border between bass and mid-range. When someone refers to "muddiness," it is often in this range. At the same time, this is the range that adds fullness and warmth to a sound, and where you find the "fat" sound for a snare drum. The upper end of this range can add clarity to bass instruments, and the lower notes of a piano or organ.

Mid-Range

(600Hz-2kHz)
This is the range that produces edge or aggressive sounds–and ear fatigue.

(500Hz-1kHz)
The effect known as "honk" lies largely in this region. It can give instruments a horn-like sound.

(800Hz)
This area can add snare, cymbal, and slap bass attack, but can also yield excessive honk.

(1kHz-2kHz)
The attack of the beater hitting a bass drum or the crack of a snare can be accentuated in this area. This is an important area for speech recognition. If boosted to excess, it can also impart a tinny or telephone-like sound.

Upper Mid-Range

(3kHz-4kHz)
This area can add attack to a bass drum beater as well as guitar attack and vocal projection. Too much can create listening fatigue and add lisping quality to vocals, where "m", "v", and "b" become indistinguishable.

The Presence Range

(4kHz-6kHz)
This area affects how near the sound seems and can help separate a sound from the rest of the mix. It adds to the clarity and definition of voices and instruments. This is the frequency range of the presence knob on a guitar amp. Too much boost can create a harsh sound.

The Treble Range

(6kHz-20kHz)
Brilliance and "air" live here. Vocal sibilance is a danger at 7kHz, but breathiness resides at around 15kHz. 7k-8kHz affects the brightness of cymbals and other high register percussion, and is often called shimmer or sizzle. Too much boost in this range can produce a metallic sound. 15k and above is more the area referred to as "air."

This track contains a drum loop. First you will hear it with the equalization flat. Then you will hear it boosted at 80Hz, then at 600Hz, then 2kHz, and finally at 7kHz. Note which parts of the drum set are affected by each boost. (The EQ returns to flat for two bars after each boost and all boosts are exaggerated for demonstration purposes.)

CHAPTER 7

GRAPHIC, PARAMETRIC, AND SHELVING EQ

What's Ahead:
- Graphic EQ
- Parametric EQ
- Shelving EQ

Equalizer effects come in a variety of types. Some of the most common are graphic, parametric, and shelving. Each has its advantages.

GRAPHIC EQ

This graphic equalizer pedal features seven bands of equalization and a master level fader to restore the volume to unity gain.

You might find a graphic equalizer on a stereo, instrument amplifier, or iTunes. It offers an individual fader for each of the frequency bands that it controls, anywhere from five or six to thirty. Pushing a fader up from a zero attenuation midpoint boosts the volume of the selected frequency, and pulling it down cuts the amount of that frequency. Low to high frequencies are arranged from left to right.

Once you have arranged the faders to modify the input signal to taste, you get to see a graphic representation of the EQ curve, hence the name. Boosting or cutting a band on the graphic equalizer does not just affect the designated band; to a certain degree, it also affects the frequencies above and below. For example, if one fader controls 500 hertz and the next fader handles 600 hertz, the 500 hertz fader may affect up to 550 hertz, while the 600 hertz fader may affect down to 551 hertz. How far afield this happens is called the "bandwidth." The more faders a graphic equalizer offers, the narrower the bandwidth of each fader. A graphic equalizer will usually have a master volume fader that allows you to restore unity gain after boosting and/or cutting the desired frequencies. Sometimes you want to be able to zero in more precisely on a particular frequency and this is where a parametric equalizer comes in.

PARAMETRIC EQ

Parametric equalizers derive their name from the fact that they offer three parameters for shaping the sound of a tone. Usually controlled by knobs (on hardware), they are a frequency selector, a cut and boost control, and a "Q" control.

- Frequency Selector: This knob chooses the frequency to be boost or cut. Some parametric equalizers will have more than one frequency selector knob, allowing you to work on more than one frequency range simultaneously. These are known as multi-band equalizers. On parametrics with more than one frequency control, the controls are often divided into ranges, with one covering low end, another mid-range, etc.

- Cut and Boost: A relatively self-explanatory control, this knob will have a center point, boosting the chosen frequency when turned clockwise, and cutting it when turned counter-clockwise.

- Q: This knob adjusts the width of the bandwidth. Narrowing the bandwidth allows you to pinpoint exact frequencies that you wish to boost or cut, then to do so while hardly affecting the frequencies surrounding it. A wider bandwidth permits a more expansive boost or cut for a more gradual effect.

As with their graphic cousins, parametric equalizers will have a control that affects the overall gain so that you can push it back up to unity gain if you have cut many of the frequencies, or bring it down if you have been mainly boosting bands.

This parametric equalizer pedal lets you zero in on very specific frequencies to boost or cut.

A wide bandwidth is described as having a "low Q," while a narrow bandwidth is described as a "high Q."

A semi-parametric EQ is a parametric EQ without the Q control. The bandwidth is set at the factory. Sometimes the Q automatically becomes higher at more extreme boost and cut settings.

SHELVING EQ

If a parametric EQ boosts or cuts only a chosen frequency, leaving most of the signal on either side of it untouched, a shelving equalizer boosts or cuts the signal starting at a particular frequency and affecting either everything above that frequency or below it.

For example, you might want to boost all the frequencies above 8kHz to add some bite and sparkle to a mix, or cut all the frequencies below 40Hz to remove any low-end rumble. The Q adjuster on shelving EQ lets you determine how radical the slope of the effect is from straight signal to boosted or cut equalization. Once the signal has been cut, it levels off into a lower or higher shelf (hence the name).

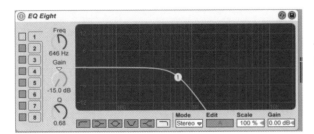

This Ableton Live EQ plug-in is set up as a shelving EQ to remove all frequencies over 646Hz.

CHAPTER 8

TONE CONTROLS

What's Ahead:

- What is a tone control?
- Passive vs. active tone controls

WHAT IS A TONE CONTROL?

This may seem like a ridiculously obvious question, but even though almost everyone has run across a tone control of some sort on a stereo, radio, or instrument amplifier, not everyone really knows exactly what they are and what they do.

In some ways, a tone control is like a parametric EQ with the Q control and the frequency selector control removed. In other words, the frequency on which it operates, as well as the bandwidth of that frequency, has been preselected by the electronics chosen for the tone control.

This form of equalization appears throughout the world of music electronics. In addition to the aforementioned stereos, radios, and instrument amplifiers, they appear on preamps, many effects pedals, and electric instruments. Some mixing boards whose channels sport knobs labeled "EQ," but no frequency selector or Q control, are essentially offering only a simple tone control.

PASSIVE VS. ACTIVE TONE CONTROLS

Tone controls come in two basic types: active and passive. The majority of tone controls are likely to be passive. Most electric guitars, basses and amplifiers employ passive tone controls.

A passive control is essentially a potentiometer with a resistor or capacitor wired to it. When fully clockwise the pot lets all of the treble, middle, or bass through. As you turn it counterclockwise, you reduce the amount of designated frequency. An active tone control uses the power from an amplifier's feedback loop, or a dedicated amplifier to actively boost certain frequencies. In some passive tone amplifiers, the amplifier does make up the lost gain from rolling off some frequencies, but is not actively boosting them. In others, turning all the tone controls down will result in no sound coming out of the amp.

Basically, a passive tone control can only reduce the relevant frequency, whereas an active tone control can decrease or increase it.

CHAPTER 9

FILTERS

What's Ahead:

- What is a filter?
- Types of filters
- Filter modulation

WHAT IS A FILTER?

Whenever you change the frequency response of a signal, you are said to be filtering it, so technically speaking, all the forms of equalization we have mentioned so far are filters. When referring more specifically to "filters," a more radical adjustment of frequency is implied. Whereas an equalizer adjusts certain frequencies by boosting or cutting them, leaving the unaffected frequencies alone, a filter can completely remove all but the desired bandwidth.

TYPES OF FILTERS

Filters come in four basic types: high pass, low pass, band pass, and notch.

- High pass: A high pass filter lets only the sound above a selected frequency through. Think of it as just allowing the treble to pass.
- Low pass: A low pass filter lets just the bass through, in other words, all the frequencies below the chosen point. A guitar tone control is a simple lowpass filter.
- Band pass: With a band pass filter, you choose the frequency, with almost everything on either side of it silenced.
- Notch: Think of a notch filter as the opposite of a bandpass, you choose the frequency to be silenced, and everything on either side is permitted to pass through unaffected.

When working with filters, in addition to the control that lets you choose the frequency, you will come across a control marked "resonance." In a bandpass or notch filter, this control acts much like the Q control on a parametric EQ. With high pass and low pass filters at higher values, it introduces a resonant peak at the chosen frequency cutoff point, giving a vocal effect to the sound. At lower values, it acts more like Q control, adjusting the slope of the cutoff.

FILTER MODULATION

While filters are often used without any modulation to statically shape the sound, we tend to be more familiar with modulated filters, where the filter shaping shifts over time within a certain range (low pass, high pass, etc.). Guitarists are most familiar with filtering stompboxes by Boss, MXR, Mu-Tron, Electro-Harmonix, Moog, and others that create the "wah" or "ow" sounds in funky music. These employ the same principles as the more complex filters in synthesizers.

Either an envelope or an LFO most commonly modulates filters. We have discussed these terms before as applied to volume, but let us look at them as employed with filters.

As with volume, a filter's envelope can consist of attack, decay, sustain and release (ADSR). Also important is the velocity control, sometimes called "amount" or "sensitivity." Pedals and plug-ins may have fewer controls and they might be labeled differently, but these parameters are essentially what they control. Synthesizers will have the full range modifiers and more, including key and envelope.

- Attack: This determines how quickly the filtering kicks in. A long attack time combined with a long decay time creates a "wah" sound.
- Decay: The length of the decay controls how quickly the filtering falls off. A long attack, combined with a short decay, gives more of a "wow" sound, while a short attack and long decay will create an "ow" effect.
- Sustain: Once the frequency falls back down, this determines the frequency at which the sound will continue.
- Release: This determines how quickly the frequency will fall off to its lowest point once the key of a synth has been released.
- Key: This adjusts how much the filtering will change as the notes move up or down the keyboard.
- Envelope: It is here that you adjust how much the envelope is affected by the strength of the input signal. On pedals, this control may be labeled "sensitivity."

This track demonstrates a filter sweeping a synthesizer note up (wah), then up and down (wow), then down (ow).

LFOs can sweep the filter up and down automatically. How quickly the tone rises and falls from bass to treble and back is determined by a control labeled "rate" or sometimes "frequency." Often, the rate of the LFO can be synchronized with the tempo, either by tapping a button, thru MIDI, or by direct synchronization with digital recording software. The character of the rise and fall is colored by the selection of different waveforms for the LFO.

Among others these may include:
- Sign: This gives a smooth, equal rise and fall with a soft peak.
- Triangle: This wave offers an equal rise and fall, but with a sharper peak.
- Saw (or sawtooth): A saw wave can either offer a quick rise and slow fall, or a slow rise and quick fall.
- Square: This wave creates a choppy effect, similar to slicing.
- Pulse (or rectangular): This is like a square wave, but the peak and valley times are not equal.
- Sample and Hold: This is a random wave with changing values stepping up and down.

This track features a simple square wave running through a filter being modified by an LFO. The LFO first uses a sine wave, followed in succession by a triangle wave, a square wave, a saw up, a saw down, and finally, a sample and hold wave.

CHAPTER 10
FILTER PEDALS

> *What's Ahead:*
> - What is a filter pedal?
> - Different types of filter pedals

WHAT IS A FILTER PEDAL?

In order for musicians to control filtering effects while continuing to use both hands on their instruments, the effects have to be placed on the floor, where nimble feet can turn them on and off, and control the sweep of the filters.

Filtering began as a combination of the equalization on mixing boards and the modification of electronic sound waves by early experimental musicians. In addition, by simply statically modifying the tone of an instrument with filters, musicians found that sweeping through the filter's peak range as they played, created an exciting and emotional sound. Sweeping the filter created both textural and rhythmic effects. With the invention of the electric guitar, bass, and piano, performing musicians developed a yen for these new sounds. Their use of effects influenced acoustic musicians like woodwind players and violinists, who, with the invention of contact microphones and pickups, were able to run through filters as they competed with wailing guitars. Once available in pedal form, filter sweeping branched out from experimental electronic music and adapted into jazz, rock, and funk.

DIFFERENT TYPES OF FILTER PEDALS

Filter pedals fall into three basic categories: Wah-wahs, Envelope Filters, and Auto Wahs.

Wah-wah pedal

You are no doubt familiar with the wah-wah pedal; it is probably the most recognized guitar effect pedal; from the "Theme from Shaft" to "Sweet Child o' Mine," popular music abounds with this uniquely human sound. Essentially a rocker pedal, an on/off switch, and an active tone control, when rocked from the heel toward the toe, it makes the vocal "wah" sound from whence it derives its name.

While testing a tone circuit for a new Vox solid-state amplifier, some engineers were sweeping the tone of an oscilloscope signal back and forth. A guitarist, Del Casher, was present at the time and encouraged Vox to release it as a guitar effect. Instead, they marketed it as a device to imitate a trumpet mute so they could sell it (and amplifiers) to woodwind players. Vox even named the first model after trumpeter Clyde McCoy.

Though sometimes considered a pedal-operated tone control, a wah pedal is actually an active band pass or low pass filter that is foot-controlled. A preamp boosts a filter peak from about 400Hz to 2.2kHz, depending on where the foot treadle is in its sweep. Most often, the treadle controls

a potentiometer attached to a gear. A ferrite core inductor creates the resonant peak that is swept by rocking the pedal. This peak is normally set to a narrow Q, or bandwidth, but some pedals allow you to adjust the Q for different types and degrees of vocalization. The many brands and models of wah-wah can sound very different from each other. Much of this difference comes from the type of inductor used.

The Cry Baby pedal is one of the most popular models of wah-wah pedal. The footswitch that allows you to turn it on and off is visible.

Much voodoo has arisen about the "best" inductor for a wah pedal. As I indicated in the introduction, and will many more times throughout this book: Use your ears and decide for yourself which sound you like, rather than accepting the current gear geek wisdom. No less a tone guru than Robben Ford uses a standard off-the-shelf wah-wah.

Envelope Filter Pedal

The terminology can get confusing when it comes to envelope filters and auto filters (or auto wahs). Boss made four different pedals in these two categories, some of which overlap between envelope and auto functions, as do models by other manufacturers.

An envelope filter sweeps frequencies much like a wah pedal, but does so in response to the amount of input that it sees. This means that if you hit your guitar or bass string, or electric piano key softly, the sweep

This small envelope filter allows you to blend a dry signal in with the filtered one.

is less than if you hit it hard. Softer hits do not produce as much treble as harder hits. Think of the envelope voltage as an invisible hand that turns the frequency knob up and down every time you play a note. Some pedals have expression inputs so that you can turn your envelope pedal into a wah. Others have switches to choose up or down sweeps, "wah" or "ow." A sensitivity control adjusts the response of the pedal to your attack.

This envelope filter allows you to choose whether the filtered sound goes up (ow) or down (wah).

Auto Filter or Auto Wah

The operative word in Auto Filter or Auto Wah is "auto," as in automatic. These pedals provide an LFO to sweep the wah up and down at an adjustable rate. Rather than one sweep per attack, like an envelope filter, an auto filter keeps going like a tremolo. This can be combined with an envelope function in some pedals; in this case, the strength of the attack will affect the initial sweep, but will level off to the control of the LFO. A few pedals allow you to adjust the LFO tempo by tapping.

On this Auto Wah there is a control for the rate of the LFO.

extras

Pedal filters can offer a few simple controls or a host of them, including frequency and resonance cutoffs, filter types (high pass, band pass, etc.), distortion, and more.

try this

A bit of distortion after the filter helps bring out the effect. Try placing an overdrive after the filter in your effects chain.

audio tracks 12

On this track you will hear a guitar played first through a filter controlled by its pick attack, then by an LFO, and then by both.

Resonance, envelope speed, and built-in distortion are just some of the extra features on this Moogerfooger pedal.

CHAPTER 11
EQ, WAH, FILTER, AND TONE TIPS

What's Ahead:
- EQ tips
- Wah tips
- Filter tips
- Tone control tips

EQ TIPS

Whether live or on a recording, equalization is an essential factor in determining the impact of your sound.

Tip 1: *Get Physical*

The most important thing to remember when dealing with EQ is the rule of physics that essentially says: *two things cannot occupy the same space at the same time.* If you put too much bass on the guitar, it is going to compete with the bass guitar. If the bass and the bass drum are in the same frequency range, the bottom will be muddy rather than punchy. If you soloed some of the individual parts in a well-produced record, you would find that by themselves they sound awful, but when mixed into the track, they are distinctly audible and serve to make the "whole" sound great.

> Listen to popular records and note how the bass often has almost no highs or mids, yet you can hear it clearly. Alone in its frequency range, it is more audible, while the bass drum might have the low end rolled off to provide the punch.

> *At the start of this track, the bass drum has the lows rolled off and the mids boosted, while the bass has the highs rolled off and the mids lowered a bit. Then the bass is panned right and the bass drum panned left so you can hear the individual EQ. When the full track returns, I remove the bass drum EQ. Note how the bass notes are less distinct. For the last two bars, the EQ is reinstated.*

> This same principle applies in a live situation. That full-frequency tone that sounds so good in your bedroom is likely to compete with many of the other instruments on stage. During rehearsals, it is important to find your place in the mix and emphasize "your" frequencies while reducing the ones that compete with other instruments.

Tip 2: *Get Radical*

Don't be afraid to get drastic with the knobs. Sometimes rolling off not just some, but all of the highs, mids, or lows, can create the interesting sound that jumps out of the mix or makes it come together. Stephen Stills' solo on the Crosby, Stills and Nash tune, "Wooden Ships," is as memorable for the dark tone created by eliminating his high end, as for anything he played. Many vintage Fender amps don't sound good until you roll the bass almost off. Don't look at numbers, use your ears. If it sounds good, it is good.

Tip 3: *Consider Your Surroundings*

When recording, a proper room and speakers (for monitoring) are necessary to ensure that you are getting an accurate picture of the sound. Even with the best environment, a great mastering engineer is essential to ensure that the overall EQ of your track will work through any speakers and in any environment.

A single, overall EQ needs to work in all environments for a recording, but when performing live, flexibility is the order of the day. Do not get locked into specific settings for your instrument and amplifier. Dark, absorbent rooms may require more treble, while a boomy gym may mean that you must radically reduce your low end.

WAH TIPS

If you must, you may rock a wah-wah pedal back and forth on quarter notes as if you were tapping the time, but I call this the "Tonight Show" technique, after that TV show's early guitarists. In the 1960s, these older players were clueless as to how to use a wah-wah but thought it might make the music more appealing to the "young folk." Here are some tips on how to get more out of your foot wagging.

Tip 1: *Rockin' in Rhythm*

Quarter note rocking can work if your hand-played rhythm is extremely funky, or occasionally to build into a musical section like a chorus or a breakdown. More often you will want to try some of these patterns:

- Rock slowly forward for two beats, then quickly back and slowly forward for the next two beats.
- Rock quickly forward on one, stay there until three, then quickly rock back and forward on four.

These all presuppose that you are playing a chordal or single note rhythm that is at least minimally funky to begin with.

Tip 2: *Vocalize*

Any good instrumental solo should have an element of "singing" to it, and a properly used wah pedal can help you make that singing more human sounding. The wah pedal is supposed to mimic the formants of speech. Some "talk" pedals actually use more vocal-sounding filters. A good solo should also contain some combination of staccato (short) and legato (long) notes. Try keeping the pedal back for some short notes then move it forward at medium speed for each long note. This should introduce a vocal element to the solo. With practice, you will begin to feel the best places to move the pedal forward and back to achieve the most realistic singing sound.

Tip 3: *Placement*

The wah-wah pedal should be toward the beginning of a pedal chain. It can come before or after overdrive and distortion, but this will have audibly different results.

- Before the distortion: This filters the signal that the distortion pedal or overdriven amp receives. Different frequencies will make the distortion circuits react differently; the sound and amount of distortion will change depending on where the pedal is along its rocking path. This is the way many rock guitarists employ wah-wah.
- After the distortion: This filters the distortion more like a synthesizer. The distortion pedal (wah is rarely placed after amp distortion) receives a consistent signal from the instrument so the basic sound and amount of the overdrive remain the same, only the tone changes.

Feel free to experiment. If you want to place a wah after your delay to filter the delays, go for it.

Tip 4: *Go Off Half-Cocked*

A wah pedal can act as an external tone knob if you turn it on and leave it in a single position along the treadle path. This is the secret to some great rock tones from bands like Thin Lizzy, the Scorpions, and Dire Straits ("Money For Nothing"). This has led to some specialty pedals with no rocker, just a knob that lets you select the wah-like frequency you desire when the pedal is engaged.

This track demonstrates the wah-wah pedal, first being used in a rhythmic fashion and then for a solo in an expressive vocal fashion.

FILTER TIPS

We learned that filters are essentially a form of extreme EQ. If traditional roots music (country, blues, bluegrass), jazz, or classical is your thing, you probably won't get involved much with filtering as an effect. But if you are into updating the aforementioned genres, or deal in electronic, dance, or modern pop music, filters are your friend.

Tip 1: *Placement*

When using an envelope filter, it is important to put it at the start of the chain. This is because it will respond to the dynamics of your playing. Compressors, overdrives, and distortions, all of which come toward the beginning of the chain, will limit the dynamics of your signal, so you want to put the envelope filter between your instrument and these pedals.

Wahs and envelope filters should always come after vintage fuzz pedals (and their clones), as these pedals need to receive a direct signal from the guitar to work properly.

Auto-filters can go in a variety of places. Radical routing, like sending a delayed signal to one side of the stereo field and a dry signal to the other side, while filtering just the delay, can create exciting effects.

Tip 2: *Spacey Trem*

Auto-filters can make an ear-catching alternative to typical tremolo. Matching the sweep to the tempo of the tune adds to the rhythmic drive. Make sure your choice of cutoff keeps the part from encroaching on the frequency range of other instruments.

Tip 3: *Filter Taming*

Unlike most tone controls or wahs, filters can create frequency boosts and resonances that can damage speakers, and more importantly, ears. When playing around with filters you will be emphasizing frequencies as often as cutting them; make sure you start at a low volume, and consider putting a compressor or limiter after the filter to tame any spikes.

TONE CONTROL TIPS

Though not as sophisticated as graphic or parametric EQs, tone controls can play a big part in shaping your sound.

Tip 1: *Ear Training*

The most important concept, and one that you will find reiterated through this book, is to use your ears! Don't be afraid to get radical with the tone knobs on your instrument or amplifier. Many old Fender amps sound horribly boomy unless you turn the bass as low as 2. If a clean, almost-acoustic tone is what you seek for your electric guitar, you might have to turn the mid-range control of your amp down near zero.

Tip 2: *Strat Mod*

The tone control next to the volume knob on a Fender Stratocaster that affects the middle pickup is not commonly used; consider having the guitar rewired so this control rolls treble off on the Strat's sometimes harsh bridge pickup instead (this also puts it near your pinky for the effect below). Leave the remaining tone control to color the neck pickup. Another modification is to wire both tone controls as master tones, operating on all three pickups, but with different capacitors on each to create different coloring.

Tip 3: *Wah-sup*

With a little practice (and finger stretching), the tone control on a Fender Telecaster or a modified Strat can be manipulated for some great crying wah effects.

Tip 4: *Balancing Act*

On Gibson guitars, like Les Pauls and 335s, or guitars with similar wiring, the availability of separate volume and tone controls for each pickup can help produce a wide variety of sounds from a single guitar. Watch old clips of B.B. King on YouTube, and you will see him constantly adjusting these knobs while playing. With the pickup switch selected for both pickups on at the same time, subtle tonal variations can be achieved by adjusting the individual volume and tone knobs.

Tip 5: *Woman Tone*

There are various ways to get the famous Eric Clapton "Woman Tone" effect, but they all require playing through a distorted amp while rolling a pickup's tone completely off. If you have a two-pickup guitar, you can play through both the neck and the bridge pickups as long as you roll both tones off. There are other cool sounds to be had by using both pickups and just rolling the tone off of one.

 On this track, you will first hear a distorted guitar lick played on a guitar with its neck pickup on and the tone full up. Then you will hear the lick played with the neck pickup's tone rolled off. Following that will be both pickups on, then both pickups with the neck tone rolled off, then with just the bridge tone rolled off. Finally, you will hear the bridge pickup, then the bridge pickup with its tone rolled off.

SECTION 3

Distortion

CHAPTER 12
AMPLIFIERS

What's Ahead:

- What is distortion?
- Tube vs. Solid-State distortion
- Power amp distortion
- Preamp distortion
- Modeled amps

WHAT IS DISTORTION?

Distortion occurs when the original shape of an object, sound, or waveform is altered. In the case of a hi-fi system, instrument amplifier, mixing board, effects pedal, rack unit, or anything else that employs an amplification stage, this alteration occurs when the amplifier reaches a level at which it can no longer increase the output signal without altering the input signal. Once the output level passes this stage, it is said to introduce distortion. The introduction of distortion to an audio signal can have the effect of adding harmonic content or overtones that did not exist in the original signal.

Distortion can add different types of harmonics. Even harmonic overtones tend to be consonant or "pleasing," while odd harmonic overtones are dissonant or "unpleasant."

Distortion acts like a compressor. As with a compressor, the more that you compress your signal, the less dynamic range you will have. If you want to maintain the expressive possibilities of hard and soft attack, be sure to go easy on the amount of distortion you use.

In a home stereo system, clean buffer pedal, or mixing board, too much distortion is not normally considered desirable. The idea is that the output signal will be identical to the input signal, only louder. Still, a slight amount of even harmonic distortion in those applications often adds a desirable effect that becomes identified as "warmth." In a guitar amplifier, larger amounts of harmonic distortion are more often welcome.

When an amplifier exceeds its upper limit of clean output, it is said to be *clipping*. There are two basic types of clipping: hard and soft.

- Hard clipping is when the amplifier abruptly hits its upper limit, going immediately from undistorted to distorted, flattening out the peak of the signal. Imagine turning a sine wave into a square wave.
- Soft clipping is less abrupt than hard clipping. The distortion begins gradually, near the upper limit. The peaks are squeezed down as opposed to lopped off.

Distortion is commonly associated with rock guitar, but it is an effect that can be used in a wide variety of situations from mild to wild.

The use of distortion as an effect has given rise to many stories about who the "first" guitarist was to use it. Tales of loose and lost tubes, or slashed speakers that led to the "discovery" of amplifier distortion are apocryphal at best. Guitar amplifiers have always distorted. Check out jazz guitarist Charlie Christian's work with Bennie Goodman in the 1940s, and you will hear a beautiful, if mild, overdriven tone that gave his guitar a horn-like quality to match his horn-style single-note playing. Rock and blues guitarists upped the distortion ante in the 1950s. It can be said that modern guitar amplifier distortion standards were set by Eric Clapton's work on the first John Mayall *Blues Breakers* record.

This is a Marshall Combo, much like the one that Eric Clapton used to revolutionize the sound of rock guitar on the *Blues Breakers* record.

TUBE VS. SOLID-STATE DISTORTION

In most arenas (guitar amps, audiophile amps, even recording gear), tube distortion has, for years, generally been believed to have a "magic" lacking in solid-state amps. While this attitude has softened in recent years, to better understand the potential applications of each, it is worth examining the difference.

The main difference is that tube distortion is a result of soft clipping, whereas early solid-state distortion was created with hard clipping. It was believed (not entirely correctly) that tube distortion created only even harmonics while solid-state distortion produced odd harmonics.

Tube amps also exhibit a quality called *sag*. Sag refers to the drooping of the power supply voltage in response to large transient signals, which lends a dynamic "feel" to the tube amplifier that is often lacking in solid-state amplifiers.

While most guitarists still prefer tube amplifiers, many of these same players will use a solid-state overdrive or distortion pedal like the Ibanez Tube Screamer (which contains no tube) or the ProCo Rat. Solid-state technology has come a long way since the invention of transistors, and the current crop of solid-state amps sound much better than the earlier models. Tastes have also changed, with some heavy metal players reveling in the gnarly odd-order harmonics and tight low-end of solid-state amps, and electronic musicians employing digital distortion, once considered an absolute no-no.

Tube Amp Pros
- "Warm" sound
- Natural compression
- Sag

Tube Amp Cons
- High weight to power ratio
- Tubes are inconsistent and unreliable
- Expensive
- High heat production
- Fragile

Solid State Amp Pros
- Low weight to power ratio
- Reliable
- Lower heat production
- Tight low-end
- Inexpensive

Solid State Amp Cons
- Less dynamic feel
- Less "natural" sound
- Harder to repair

The Fender Twin Reverb is a classic tube amplifier that is valued for its warm clean sound. It is rarely used for distortion without some kind of pedal.

Some amps are a hybrid of tube and solid-state. They may have a tube preamp and solid-state power section, or less often, a solid-state preamp and a tube power amp.

POWER AMP DISTORTION

An instrument amplifier takes the signal from the instrument's pickup(s) and raises it to a level that can drive the speakers, and is audible to the audience. The main work is performed by one to eight tubes called the power tubes. But before they can do their job, the signal must be raised to a level that these tubes can recognize; this job falls to the preamp tube(s). Most guitarists agree that when it comes to tube amplifier distortion, the best way to create it is to drive the power tubes by turning up the amplifier. This has one significant drawback: An amplifier will produce its optimum distortion tone within a very small volume range. Push the tubes too hard, and the sound can get mushy and indistinct; don't push it hard enough and the sound will be too clean. You might think, no problem, find that range and always play there. Unfortunately, for many musicians this is not an option. Depending on the output of the amplifier, the optimum volume may be too loud for some rooms and not loud enough for others. There are a number of solutions to this problem.

- Power Attenuator: A power attenuator is basically a volume control with a dummy load and a heat sink attached. It is placed between the amp's speaker output and the speaker. As you turn down the knob, the volume of the amp is reduced, even though the amp volume remains high, driving the power tubes. The dummy load makes the amp believe that it is still experiencing the full resistance of the speaker, and the heat sink soaks up any additional heat generated by this process. This can get close to a full-bore amp distortion sound, except it lacks the tonal subtleties added by speaker distortion.

- Plexiglass: Some guitarists carry a Plexiglass sheet to place in front of the amp to protect the ears of the band and the audience on smaller stages, and/or in smaller rooms.
- Multiple amplifiers: An extravagant solution is to tour with a variety of amps at different wattages and pick the right one for the room.
- Multiple cabinets: A variation that I once came up with on tour was to carry a 40-watt Fender Bandmaster head and two speaker cabinets. One was a Marshall 4x10" and the other a custom 1x12" with an Electro-Voice speaker. The head was rated 4 ohms, but each cabinet was rated 8 ohms. In small rooms, I ran the Marshall cabinet alone; the 8-ohm load acted as a kind of attenuator on the 4-ohm head. In slightly larger rooms, I would use the Electro-Voice cabinet, which, though it only had one speaker, was more efficient than the Marshall, and thus, louder. In the largest rooms, I would use both, not only giving me more speakers, but because they were attached in parallel, it reduced the speaker load to 4 ohms, thereby letting the amp deliver full power.

PREAMP DISTORTION

Starting in the 1970s, tube amp companies hit upon the idea of wiring a master volume into their products. This let the player turn up the preamp as much as they liked, while lowering the volume between the preamp and the power amp with the master. Unfortunately, the sound that this produced tended to be thin and fuzzy.

As technology progressed, preamp distortion improved to the point where it approached the richness of power amp overdrive. This varies greatly from amplifier to amplifier, but is fortunately easy enough to check on before purchasing in person, whether in a store or second-hand. If you buy online, make sure the product is returnable in the event that the sound is not acceptable.

The Vox AC30 is a tube amp, prized for its distinctive power-tube crunch when turned up to rock and roll volumes.

MODELED AMPS

The advent of cheaper, smaller, faster, and more powerful computing chips brought with it the advent of amplifier modeling in both hardware and software form. We will delve further into this subject in the Modeling chapter, but here we will discuss the distortion aspects.

origins

The new Millennium introduced an explosion of digital modeling. Line 6 introduced amp modeling software late in the last century with Amp Farm. The fact that it was only available to high-end Pro Tools TDM users initially limited the spread of the modeling concept. Line 6's introduction of the hardware POD a few years later started a modeling revolution when players realized that they could get realistic amp tones in their bedrooms late at night. The rise of home recording greatly encouraged other companies to get on the bandwagon.

Modeled amps, whether in software or hardware form, behave much like their real world counterparts. A model of a Fender Twin is not going to provide a heavy-metal-style distortion sound on its own, while a Marshall model is unlikely to offer a warm, rounded, clean tone for jazz. As of this writing, modeled amps tend to do extremes better than subtleties; that is, many offer acceptable clean tones or ripping shred sounds, while fewer are

Line 6's Amp Farm was the first widely adopted amp modeling software, appearing on more recordings than you might think.

capable of realistic mild crunch tones and smooth edge of breakup solo sounds. One tip is to add a modeled overdrive or booster to the amp model to achieve these more delicate nuances.

On this track, recorded using Ableton Live, you will hear a guitar played through a plug-in model of an overdriven guitar amp, and then a real overdriven guitar amp that has been mic'd and recorded. The modeling was done in Native Instruments Guitar Rig 3 using their Vox amp model, driven by their Ibanez Tube Screamer model, and a Boss Compressor model, through the Guitar Rig delay and reverb models. The real amp was an Egnater Rebel 30, driven by a Blackstone Appliances Mosfet overdrive, using the Ableton Live Filter Delay and Overloud Breverb plug-in.

The red, kidney-bean-shaped Line 6 POD spread the modeling gospel like wildfire when it came out. It remains a popular tool for both recording and live applications.

CHAPTER 13

BOOSTERS

What's Ahead:

- Pedal distinctions: boost vs. overdrive vs. distortion vs. fuzz
- Clean boosters
- Colored boosters
- Booster overdrives

PEDAL DISTINCTIONS: BOOST VS. OVERDRIVE VS. DISTORTION VS. FUZZ

When it comes to distortion, especially as it refers to pedals, the terminology can be confusing. Technically, any device that changes your clean signal into a dirty one is a distortion device. More commonly, the various terms like boost, overdrive, distortion and fuzz, refer to degrees and sonic qualities of distortion.

As with many definitions, these terms can be flexible. I will get into the finer points when I cover each type in its own chapter, but for now:

- Boost pedals are used for a louder clean sound, or to push an amplifier into distorting, or to increase already existing distortion.
- Overdrives create a mild distortion where none existed.
- Devices labeled "distortion" create more extreme, less dynamic grit than overdrives.
- Fuzz pedals create a gritty, radical distortion that bears little relation to the sound of an over-driven amp.

origins

The original booster was a set of highly overwound pickups on a guitar. Before the days of pedals, guitarists would install DiMarzio Super Distortion pickups in their instruments, and these monsters would drive the front end of the amp into distortion.

CLEAN BOOSTERS

A clean booster pedal is like a switchable buffer preamp that increases the output gain a bit, without coloring the signal. Some musicians like to solo with a clean sound but prefer to keep their instrument volume up full at all times. For these players, a clean boost pedal allows them to increase their volume without changing the volume setting on their instrument. Others might use it to drive the front end of the amp into distortion or increase the distortion on an already-overdriven amp by significantly increasing the output gain of the boost pedal. A clean boost allows them to maintain the tonal characteristics of both their instrument and amp while doing so. A clean booster pedal needs only one knob labeled "volume," or "gain."

The MXR Micro Amp was one of the original clean booster pedals. It increases the output of an instrument without adding distortion or excessive tonal coloration.

COLORED BOOSTERS

Sometimes you might want a darker or brighter sound for your solos. A coloring booster might allow you to simultaneously cut or boost the highs as you boost the signal. This type of pedal can help make single-coil pickups sound like humbuckers, and vice-versa. These are not called "colored boosters" per se, but might be called a "treble boost," "fat boost," or just "preamp." A colored booster might have two knobs, one for volume and one for tone, or use a switch for the tonal variations.

This booster made by 65 amps offers a range
of tonal coloration in addition to boost.

Early so-called "treble boosters" actually boosted a wide range of frequencies in addition to treble. The Treble Booster moniker appended to devices by Dallas Rangemaster and Vox was a marketing tool to entice guitarists looking to cut through a mix.

BOOSTER OVERDRIVES

Technically, a clean or colored booster will not add any distortion of its own, but many so-called booster pedals include a knob that will add grit. To be an actual booster and not an overdrive, turning this knob all the way down should remove any added distortion.

One advantage of some booster overdrive pedals is that you can leave them on (if you wish) and clean up your signal by backing off your instrument volume.

Here is a booster pedal driving a clean amp into distortion, then increasing the distortion on an already overdriven amp.

If a booster doesn't add any drive of its own, the only way to add drive to a clean amp is to make it significantly louder. If you are using it to increase the drive of an already dirty amp, the amp's compression will prevent the volume difference from being as extreme.

CHAPTER 14

OVERDRIVES

BOOSTER OR OVERDRIVE: WHAT IS THE DIFFERENCE?

As we mentioned in the last chapter, some booster pedals will have a section that adds overdrive to your signal. In fact, there is a certain amount of overlap between boost and overdrive effects. The main difference is one of emphasis:

- A booster pedal should primarily raise the level of the input to your amplifier by a significant amount–enough to push the amp set clean into distortion. If it offers an overdrive section at all, the amount should be minimal.

- An overdrive pedal may provide a fair amount of boost, but it should primarily provide an acceptable, natural (meaning amp-like), overdriven sound, even with the amp clean and unboosted.

The original Ibanez TS-808 Tube Screamer, and its immediate successor, the TS9, are generally considered to be unofficial benchmarks for overdrive pedals. These pedals add a bit of boost and a slight overdrive that has been valued for helping to create a smooth, yet aggressive distortion when combined with a slightly overdriven amp. This sound, along with a fair amount of subjective "voodoo" imparted by blues/rock legend Stevie Ray Vaughan's use, has launched a staggering number of imitations and "improvements." Companies seeking to improve on the original lament the vintage pedal's lack of low end and over-compression. Of course, these two qualities may be part of what has made these pedals so coveted. At the volumes that they are often employed, low end can build up quickly and turn into mud. The compression that a Tube Screamer adds can help add sustain and even out some rough playing.

Overdrive effects evidence soft clipping (see Chapter 12) and strive for the warm, tube-like tone of an overdriven amplifier. Like an amplifier, they should clean up when you back off the volume of your instrument. If you want to go from a crystal-clear amp sound to a hard rock, metal, or fuzz-style distortion, an overdrive is not for you, but for blues, classic rock and certain styles of jazz, an overdrive pedal is just the thing. With the drive part rolled back, it can sometimes be used to warm up drums, keyboards, and vocals as well.

The Ibanez TS 808 Tube Screamer is something of a standard for overdrive pedals, the originals prized for a particular chip used in the circuit.

Early TS9 Tube Screamers used the exact same chip as the 808; later ones switched to the one used in the reissues. If you can hear the difference (and care), be prepared to pay collector's prices.

Here is a track with an overdrive in front of a clean amp. First you will hear the clean amp, then the overdrive with the guitar volume full up, then the overdrive with the guitar volume backed off. (The recorded volume has been raised on the last section so that you can hear clearly that the sound is cleaner.)

TO TUBE OR NOT TO TUBE

In the 1980s, BK Butler developed an overdrive that employed a 12AX7 preamp tube to help impart a more "natural" sounding breakup. Guitarists (and tone fanatics) Eric Johnson and David Gilmour adopted this Tube Driver as part of their sound. Other manufacturers followed with varying degrees of success.

The concept proved as susceptible to the fads and fashions of guitar tone as any other pedal design, and for a while, tube-driven distortion pedals were nowhere to be seen. As of this writing, Mr. Butler is back with a limited amount of Tube Drivers, and other companies are once again offering pedals driven by 12AX7 and even tiny Nuvistor tubes.

If the use of an actual tube to create tube distortion is such an obvious idea, why doesn't it rule the overdrive roost? For one thing, glass tubes are fragile, and between transportation and foot stomping, a floor pedal can take a lot of abuse. For another, we are talking about a preamp tube here, and as we have learned, power tube distortion is a more highly coveted sound. Using power tubes to drive a pedal is apparently not possible, but there are non-tube pedals that approximate this sound fairly accurately. Still, many continue to feel that a tube is the best producer of tube distortion, so there will always be a market for these types of pedals, whether they are new or used.

PEDAL VS. AMP

There are few guitarists who will claim that the overdrive from a pedal sounds better than that from a high-quality tube amp. Still, the vast majority of guitarists use some sort of overdrive pedal. There are many reasons for this.

- Many guitarists play through something less than the highest quality amplifier. A good overdrive pedal will sound much better than a so-so amp—especially when it comes to mild distortion. Even an expensive boutique pedal is much cheaper than an expensive boutique or vintage amp.

- Effects like chorus, delay, and reverb sound better coming after overdrive. Many amps—even high-quality ones—lack an effects loop that would allow you to place these ambient effects after the overdrive stage of the amp. Placing them after an overdriven power stage is even more problematic (though not impossible, as we will see in the advanced section). A good overdrive pedal is easily placed in front of these effects in the floor chain.

- An overdrive pedal quickly turns a one-channel amp into the equivalent of a two-channel amp (and a two-channel amp into a three-channel version). It allows you to set the amp clean and instantly access a distorted sound with a stomp of your foot, or set one channel of a two-channel amp for clean and the other for a slight breakup, using the pedal for two additional sounds, depending on which channel is selected, for a total of four possible levels of breakup.

- Achieving distortion with an amplifier may require playing at a volume that is too loud for the venue. An overdrive pedal is an alternative to a power attenuator in the quest to get the breakup you want, at any volume you like.

The Hermida Zendrive pedal sounds so much like an incredibly expensive boutique Dumble amp that tone-meister Robben Ford occasionally leaves his Dumble at home and plays through a Zendrive into a Fender Twin Reverb.

CHAPTER 15

DISTORTION

What's Ahead:

- What is the difference between overdrive and distortion?
- Distortion flavors
- How much distortion is too much?

WHAT IS THE DIFFERENCE BETWEEN OVERDRIVE AND DISTORTION?

As we mentioned in the section on overdrive, distortion implies a harder clipping of the input signal. Here, the peak of the waveform is chopped off radically and abruptly.

Before the invention of high gain amps like the Mesa Boogie Rectifier or the Soldano, distortion pedals were the only way to get the particular kind of buzz saw breakup that is popular with harder rock and metal bands. Early pedals, like the MXR Distortion+ and the ProCo Rat, allowed guitarists to emulate the extremely aggressive sound of a high-watt amp on 10.

It is less likely that a distortion pedal will clean up when you back your instrument volume down, though it's not impossible. There is a fair amount of crossover between overdrives and distortions, just as there are between overdrives and boosters at the other end of the scale. A distortion pedal may or may not offer significant boost, but a certain amount is desirable, for reasons that we will discuss in the next section.

This track first features a clean amp sound, then an overdrive pedal, and then a distortion pedal. I have tried to keep the amount of breakup similar so you can hear the qualitative rather than the quantitative difference in the sound.

DISTORTION FLAVORS

While overdrives fall into essentially two categories, American (i.e., Fender) and British (i.e., Vox or Marshall), distortion pedals come in these, as well as a variety of other types. Since they do not necessarily attempt to emulate a particular amp or genre of amp, they are free to represent a rainbow of tonal colors. Some might go for a natural amp sound, whether a smooth Dumble or a maxed-out Rectifier. Others may revel in a more artificial rasp and push the edge of the fuzz spectrum. As of this writing, the Boss effects company alone offers five different distortion pedals, and that doesn't count a couple of overdrives that overlap into distortion mode. A quick perusal of an online equipment site reveals over fifty pedals that lay claim to distortion.

If this seems daunting, well it is! Guitarists spend their entire careers sifting through pedal after pedal looking for the

The Pro Co Rat is a classic distortion pedal that can range from almost overdrive to nasty rasp.

elusive one that speaks in their voice. Fortunately, you can be guided, to a certain extent, by the pedal's name and description. If you are looking for a more natural, rootsier sound, you probably want to stay away from a pedal labeled "Zombie Rectified Distortion" pedal. On the other hand, if a classic 60s or 70s tone is what you seek, something called "Box of Rock" might be a good place to start. Still, be prepared for surprises. You might suspect that a pedal by Coffin Case called "Blood Drive Distortion" would be a metal monster, but in fact, it turns out to be a very warm, natural distortion that might even serve for blues—go figure.

Trying before you buy is the best course, but that alone is not enough. The most experienced players will tell you that some pedals may sound terrific with one amp and awful with another. It's best to try the pedal through your own amp before you take the plunge. You might have to bring your amp to the store, but most online retailers and many stores offer 30-day return policies.

This Boss Distortion pedal offers two modes: one warmer and one harsher. A jack for an external footswitch allows you to change modes with your foot.

With distortion, as with any other effect, there is no "best" one. Part of the fun of effects is that they are like spices. You wouldn't say that cumin is better than chili powder, or pepper is better than salt. You might prefer one or the other, but they all have uses when mixed with other, compatible ingredients.

HOW MUCH DISTORTION IS TOO MUCH?

Obviously, this is a subjective question, but there are some things that might help you decide for yourself. As it clips the signal, distortion is compressing it as well. With a moderate amount of breakup, you can still get some dynamics in your playing. Attacking the note more softly will result in a quieter sound with less breakup, while hitting it harder increases the volume and grit. As you increase the gain on your amp or pedal, this is less and less the case until the strength of your attack has no effect at all on either volume or timbre. Of course, you might feel that in exchange you get a near-infinite sustain and aggressive tone. The enhanced sustain is indisputable—this is, after all, a result of the aforementioned compression. The second benefit of massive gain has come into question among some players.

Some metal-lovers seem committed to the scooped mid-range, enhanced low-end sound of a high-gain amplifier or dedicated metal pedals. But many players have come to believe that the less compressed tone of the classic rock guitarists like Jimmy Page, Jeff Beck, and Paul Kossof, is actually more aggressive, with its prominent mid-range and upper-mid bite.

Metal lovers should keep in mind that scooping the mid-range of a sound actually decreases the apparent loudness, so make sure your amp or pedal has enough boost to compensate. Whichever camp you side with, you should consider the fact that distortion tends to sit your instrument back in the mix, as well as take up a lot of sonic space. This is why many producers double distorted tracks with clean (or at least cleaner) ones to enhance articulation and presence.

On this track, I recorded the same part with a distorted guitar in the right channel and a clean one in the left channel. Note how the clean notes are much more distinguishable and jump out of the track.

CHAPTER 16
FUZZ

What's Ahead:
- What is fuzz?
- Types of fuzz
- Making fuzz musical

WHAT IS FUZZ?

To approximate the sound that a fuzz pedal makes, just say the word and extend the end: fuzzzzzzzzzz. The classic buzz-saw rasp of this pedal was among the first pedal effects. A fuzz pedal uses transistors to create a radical, hard-clipping sound, and therefore sounds nothing like tube amplifiers—no matter how distorted. Distortions and overdrives tend to use diodes and opamps to achieve the breakup, and even in the hairiest distortion pedals, the clipping is softer than in some fuzz pedals.

As with boosters, overdrives, and distortions, there is a fair amount of wiggle room in what people describe as fuzz, with some pedals doing double duty as one or more of the aforementioned. In general though, if the sound resembles any amp you have ever heard, it is more of a distortion than a fuzz. If it has a more aggressive, ragged nastiness than a distortion pedal, it is likely a fuzz.

origins

Legend has it that one of the first fuzz solos was on country artist Marty Robbins' 1961 song "Don't Worry"—the result of a broken channel in the mixing board. When other artists wanted that sound, an appropriately named engineer, Glen Snotty, came up with a transistorized pedal to produce the nasty effect. He purportedly gave the circuit to Gibson guitars, which came out with the Maestro Fuzz-Tone. It was Keith Richards' use of this pedal on 1965's "(I Can't Get No) Satisfaction" that introduced fuzz to the larger pop world.

TYPES OF FUZZ

The transistors employed in a fuzz pedal can be either germanium or silicon. Early fuzz pedals used transistors made out of germanium. It is ironic that transistors were adopted to replace the more fragile, inconsistent, unstable, and unreliable tube, yet the germanium transistor exhibits many of these same flaws. Nevertheless, germanium transistors are still valued over the silicon transistors that replaced them in many fuzz units, as they are considered less harsh and more musical sounding. Vintage germanium fuzzes can be extremely inconsistent in tone, and you would be advised to try before you buy. Modern germanium fuzz manufacturers test each transistor to make sure that the sound is consistent.

The Fuzzface, now manufactured by Dunlop, responds in some ways like an overdrive, i.e., cleaning up when the instrument volume is reduced.

Though there is no mistaking the sound of fuzz for that of an overdrive pedal, some fuzz units exhibit similar dynamic properties: cleaning up when the volume is backed off, and responding to the level of input attack. Others react differently to lowered instrument level, not cleaning up, but often distorting in a more jagged manner.

Octave fuzzes, like the Roger Mayer Octavia used by Jimi Hendrix, use a frequency doubling circuit that adds hints of an upper octave to the fundamental note.

This track features a basic fuzz sound playing rhythm and then lead, followed by an octave fuzz solo. Note how the octave becomes more pronounced when I move up the neck of the guitar and even more so when I roll off the tone part way through the second solo. I am playing the octave fuzz through a clean amp so the sound will be well defined. The thin sound you hear is often beefed up by playing octave fuzz through a distorted amp or an overdrive pedal.

The classic Big Muff was one of the earliest fuzz pedals, offering a full sound favored by Robert Fripp and Smashing Pumpkins.

Fuzz pedals fell out of favor for a time in the 1980s, but came back in the 90s as a great way to add a bit of violent pigmentation to music that was becoming perhaps too pastel. These days, there are over one hundred different fuzz pedals from which to choose, each with its own unique character.

MAKING FUZZ MUSICAL

You might find yourself plugging into your mail-order fuzz pedal, playing a few notes, and exclaiming, "This sounds terrible" (or more earthy words to that effect). Before you pack it up and return it, thinking that it's broken or that fuzz is not for you, consider that more so than boosters, overdrives, and distortions, fuzzes require a fair amount of finesse to make them reveal their tonal charms.

Step one is to make sure that there are no other pedals between the fuzz and the guitar. Most vintage-style fuzz pedals work best when they see the unadulterated level put out by your instrument. Any other pedal in the path is likely to buffer the signal causing the fuzz pedal to be unhappy. That being said, you want to attack your strings pretty hard to send the fuzz a clear and consistent input.

Some fuzz boxes sound thin and raspy, with little or no sustain when played into a clean amp. Their function is to add extra edge and color to an already distorted sound. They sound best through an overdriven amp or overdrive pedal that is turned on. This should immediately flesh out the sound of the fuzz. If it is still too trebly for your taste, feel free to roll off the tone on your instrument. This can turn a nest full of bees into a mellow, cello-like sound.

First you will hear the fuzz alone, then the fuzz played through an overdrive.

The bottom line is that whatever fuzz pedal or pedals you end up choosing, you will need to experiment to find the settings that yield the most satisfying tone.

BIT REDUCTION AND DOWNSAMPLING

What's Ahead:

- What are bit and sample rates?
- What is bit reduction and downsampling?
- Why would I want to sound like that?

WHAT ARE BIT AND SAMPLE RATES?

If you have done any digital recording, or are interested in recorded audio at all, you have no doubt come across terms like 16 bit at 44.1kHz or 24 bit at 48kHz. These terms refer to the quality of the audio recording. The first number is the number of bits and the second number refers to the sampling rate. A short and necessarily basic explanation of bits and sampling rates is required before we explain why you might want to reduce them.

Digital sound is made up of continuous analog waveforms that are reduced to ones and zeros—the binary code upon which everything digital is based. "Bit" is short for binary digit. The bit rate (sometimes called "word length") refers to the number of bits used to represent an analog audio wave.

Increasing a sample's bit rate increases the fidelity of the recording to the original. If you picture the curve of an analog waveform and then divide that curve into steps rather than a continuous line, it becomes obvious that the more steps you have, the smaller each step becomes and the closer it reverts to being a smooth curve once again, accurately representing the analog signal.

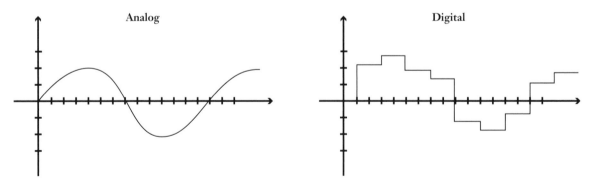

The more bits used, the more the digital wave begins to resemble the original analog wave.

The "sample" rate refers to how many times per second the waveform is being sampled. The sampling rate must be greater than twice the frequency to be reproduced for the most accurate results. These days, with sampling rates of some digital recorders reaching 19,248kHz, the accuracy of digital recordings can greatly exceed that of analog. This is great news for reproducing acoustic and electronic instruments, and the human voice, but sometimes accuracy is not what we want.

WHAT IS BIT REDUCTION AND DOWNSAMPLING?

There are a number of hardware devices and software plug-ins that will reduce the bit and/or sample rates of an audio signal. Reducing the bit rate produces digital distortion by reducing the resolution or bandwidth of digital audio data. This distortion adds overtones that turn the wave shape angular.

When a digital example of a sound is downsampled, not every sample will be processed, with the result sounding more, well, digital. The lower the sample rate the more the sound is deconstructed, and a harsh sound called "aliasing" is introduced.

WHY WOULD I WANT TO SOUND LIKE THAT?

Digital sound has improved steadily to where it is often indistinguishable from analog. That's a good thing, right? In most circumstances it is, but in the search for new sounds or the recreation of old ones, musicians have learned to embrace the oddities of bit reduction (or "bitcrushing" as it is sometimes called) and sample reduction. Nostalgia has already set in for the sound of early, lower fidelity digital devices like the Ensoniq Mirage, Fairlight CMI, and Commodore-64 computer, as well as early 6- and 8-bit computer games. Analog distortion will always be enormously popular, but some like Trent Reznor of Nine Inch Nails, revel in the more belligerent tonality of digital breakup.

Processing a signal through bitcrushing and/or downsampling hardware or software can add new colors to your sonic pallet. It can evoke the sound of seminal hip-hop recordings that employed primitive samplers, spice up drum tracks with a sci-fi rather than hi-fi sound, or create guitar tracks that go beyond "in-your-face" to "rip off your face."

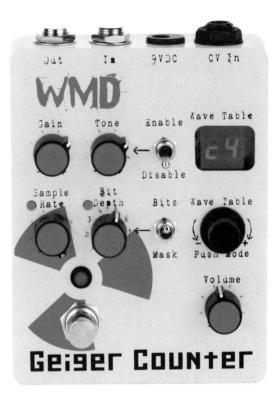

The WMD Geiger Counter offers bit reduction and downsampling in a pedal form.

On this track, I have run the guitar through some regular distortion first to fatten it up, then applied bit reduction and downsampling to deconstruct it. A little reduction has been applied to the drums to make them fit with the guitar. I have automated the downsampling on both drums and guitar for some moving, spacey effects.

SECTION **4**

Modulation

CHAPTER 18
PITCH SHIFTING

What's Ahead:

- Analog Shifting: Tape and Octavers
- Tape
- Octave fuzz
- Octave pedals
- Digital: Pitch Shifting
- Harmonization
- Pitch Correction
- Whammy effects

ANALOG SHIFTING: TAPE AND OCTAVERS

Pitch shifting is a complicated process, but to get a basic picture of how analog (or for that matter some digital) pitch shifting works, you just need to understand the relationship between pitch and time. Any sound wave is traveling over a period of time. If you shorten that period, the pitch goes up. If you lengthen it, the pitch goes down. Older readers, DJs, or new vinyl converts will relate to how the speed of the turntable can affect the sound of the record.

Owners of tape, analog, or even some digital delays can send a signal into a device set for a 500-millisecond delay with a large number of repeats. (If you have downloaded Live, put the Simple Delay plug-in into a track with a drum clip, shut off Sync, and right-click on its name bar for the menu to set it for Repitch.) As a signal travels through the delay, make the delay length longer and shorter while listening to how the pitch of a note played into the device changes. This principle is very important as it will apply to many of the forms of modulation discussed in this section.

In case you don't own a turntable or delay, check out how the pitch alters as I change the delay setting on this track.

TAPE

Today, a signal's pitch can easily be altered in any increment and to any degree by advanced digital processing, but you might be surprised to learn that pitch modification was among the earliest of electronic effects. As early as 1948, Les Paul was slowing down the tape on his recorder, laying down parts and then doubling their tempo (and their pitch) by returning the tape to its original speed. Forty years later, Fleetwood Mac's Lindsey Buckingham was using similar effects on his solo records. This is done with a process called vari-speed that involves raising or lowering the voltage being sent to the tape machine capstan, and is still occasionally used in recording studios.

Tape speed manipulation was used to create a variety of historical effects. An early method used a "wrap" (or cover) over the capstan to change its effective width. Chuck Berry's voice was sped up to make him sound younger than his thirty years. Looney Tunes icons Tweety and Daffy Duck are Mel Blanc's voice sped up to varying degrees. Hendrix's "Third Stone from the Sun" rap was his voice slowed down.

OCTAVE FUZZ

We discussed fuzz octave pedals a bit in the last chapter. Here we will delve a little further into the octave aspect of the octave fuzz. One of the earliest guitar pedals was Roger Mayer's Octavia, made famous by Jimi Hendrix on his "Purple Haze" and "Fire" solos. Originally called the "Octavio," it was a fuzz that featured an analog frequency doubling circuit, creating a hint of an octave above and along with the original note. Many emulations and versions of this effect followed.

The Fender Blender provides an upper octave and exhibits a fuzz character all its own.

On the lower strings and lower frets, this pitch shifting sounds less like an actual octave and more like a harmonic overtone. In that register, it can be used to increase the aggressive sound of the fuzz, and when applied to certain notes played together, will create metallic dissonances that some players find exciting. On the first three strings though, especially above the 12th fret, it creates a more obvious upper octave effect.

Turning the instrument's tone knob down, and thus rolling off the high end, greatly enhances this effect in any Octavia-style fuzz. This turns a subtle overtone into a sweet, flute-like sound in the upper registers. This works best with the neck pickup of a guitar. With the tone full up and the bridge pickup engaged, turning down the volume of a guitar played through octave fuzz could evoke the sound of a sitar, or bit reduction (see Chapter 17). The resulting lack of sustain only makes these sounds more authentic.

You will first hear an octave fuzz with the guitar volume full up and then with the volume backed off to evoke a sitar sound. To get a more sitar-y sound, use a light picking attack, as octave fuzz pedals are very sensitive to input.

The Boss OC-2 morphed into the OC-3, whose Poly mode restricts octaves to certain notes.

OCTAVE PEDALS

It wasn't until 1982 that a device that offered a lower octave appeared. Though you could make an octave below pedal by dividing the frequency of the original signal in half, Roland's Boss pedal division chose to create the first popular octave down pedal by repeating the fundamental while emphasizing the harmonics of the octave below and two octaves below the original signal.

Guitar players and even bassists embraced this new OC-2 pedal. Guitarists could use it to fake bass parts, removing the original signal by turning down the direct level knob, or they might just add an octave or two below to emulate synthesizers or just fatten their sound. Bassists used it to add even lower parts (this was before five-string basses) or to keep the low end going when playing up the neck.

Subsequent octave devices have used the frequency dividing method, and more recently, digital means have been employed to create the lower octaves. While the analog models are strictly monophonic (multiple simultaneous notes will create freak-outs that only the hardest core noise addict will enjoy), new digital Electro-Harmonix POG and HOG pedals allow full chords to be played with both octaves below and above.

Electro-Harmonix's POG2 pedal offers polyphonic tracking of one and two octaves above and below the original note, as well as attack decay for swells, filtering, and slight detuning effects. All of these can be stored in eight program slots.

First you will hear a faux bass part played with a POG2 octave pedal, then the lower octave combined with the original.

Like upper octave devices, lower octave pedals prefer to see a steady signal; unlike their higher kin, you can use other pedals first, though distortions work better post octave. A compressor in front of the pedal can help tracking.

Tape speed manipulation is still used by some analog diehards, and the original Octavia and Boss Octaver sound remains prized by guitarists for their richness of tone. These days though, the majority of pitch manipulation is done in the digital realm.

DIGITAL: PITCH SHIFTING

The advances in digital processing during the 1980s brought new, complex methods of pitch shifting. These might involve rapid-fire delaying of the signal, or sampling the signal and then changing its frequency. These new methods allowed sound workers to change the pitch of a signal without changing the time frame. In other words, raising or lowering the pitch of the signal an octave would no longer make the resulting music go twice or half as fast. (Conversely, it allowed music or speech to be sped up or slowed down without affecting the pitch.) Digital harmonizers can add any interval to the original signal as well as multiple octaves both up and down.

Any octave, say middle C on the piano to the next C higher, is divided into twelve half steps; intervals smaller than a half step are referred to as "cents." Each of these half steps can be further divided into 100 "cents." The current speed of digital processing permits this to take place in real time, so notes other than octaves can be shifted as they are played. More extreme pitch shifting like Whammy pedals, harmonizers, and pitch correction (Auto-Tune) will be covered in following sections, but subtle pitch alteration of just a few cents can be a valuable sonic tool as well.

During the Garth Brooks era in the early 1990s, I was playing country music in bars, trying to emulate the guitar sounds I was hearing on recordings. I thought that the guitarists were adding chorus to their solos, but when I tried that it never sounded quite right. Then I got the new-at-the-time digital Alesis Quadraverb multi-effects rack unit. In addition to delay and reverb, it featured an effect called "pitch shift" that allowed me to add a second version of my original signal that had been "detuned" up or down just a few cents. Unlike chorus, this pitch remained constant [see Chorus], creating a much less "floaty" sound. Also unlike most of the available chorus pedals at that time, the Quadraverb allowed me to blend in as much or as little of the effect as I chose. With a little experimentation, I soon had the exact sound that I was hearing on those country hits.

Digital recording lets you create this effect and many other pitch effects either with plug-ins or by directly affecting the audio (depending on the DAW). This form of slight pitch alteration is invaluable for enriching the sound of a variety of instruments and vocals, as well as creating doubling effects and widening stereo fields.

On this clip, I recorded a single mono track of guitar, then cut and pasted it to another track, panning them hard right and left. First you will hear the track with the pitch the same for both. Then you will hear the right track detuned by –10 cents. Note how it widens the stereo image.

HARMONIZATION

Once you start shifting the pitch a half step or more, you are in the realm of harmonization. The first commonly used harmonizer was digital hardware, the H910, produced by Eventide in the early 1970s. Eventide harmonizers quickly became a studio standard and have virtually dominated the field ever since. These expensive two-space rack units can also be found in the live kits of professional musicians as diverse as guitarists Trevor Rabin, Robert Fripp, and Steve Vai; trumpeter Jon Hassell; and harmonica player John Popper of Blues Traveler.

This top-of-the-line Eventide 8000 is the king of the harmonizer hardware.

Harmonizers perform the aforementioned slight pitch shifting for doubling effects, but can also provide musical intervals for harmonizing solos (see "Owner of a Lonely Heart" by Yes, p. 115), as well as significantly detuning drums for a fatter sound and adding room-rumbling lower octaves to basses. Many of the modern harmonizers will perform "smart" harmonization, rather than remaining at one set interval as you play or sing (like a third or a fifth), will shift the interval based on the musical key for which you set them. For example, set for fifths in the key of C, a smart harmonizer would know to harmonize a B with an F, rather than F♯.

Many harmonizers contain other effects like delays and filtering. These, combined with their pitch altering capabilities, can create a world of spacey effects essential to electronic and ambient music, as well as sound design for radio, television, commercials, games, and film.

The first sound you will hear on this track will be a fuzz guitar harmonized in fifths. Then you will hear a swelled note through a delay, with each repeat shifting the pitch up an octave. The snare drum is a sample with its pitch lowered by a harmonizer plug-in.

Though the top-of-the-line Eventide Harmonizer will set you back thousands of dollars, there are now pedals that offer harmonizing effects in the low hundreds. For recording, there are plug-ins (some of them free) that will perform many of these effects.

PITCH CORRECTION

Pitch shifters and harmonizers have also been used to "fix" out of tune or "wrong" notes in recording almost since their invention. There are even tape tricks that were used before the onset of digital technology. In 1997, Antares Audio Technologies introduced Auto-Tune, a plug-in that not only allowed quick, transparent, and accurate pitch correction for pre-recorded material, but also would perform this magic in real time, allowing live vocals to be cleaned up as well.

Auto-Tune uses a process known as phase vocoding that is too complex to go into here. Simply, it permits the pitch of individual notes to be shifted into the proper tuning, without distortion or artifacts. As with a smart harmonizer, you can set the key and it will make sure all the notes in the performance conform to that key.

In addition to correction, Auto-Tune and similar products like Celemony's Melodyne may be used for a vocoder-like effect (see Cher's "Believe" or tunes by T-Pain), as a harmonizer, or even to restructure previously recorded melodies into new ones. Celemony has a version of Melodyne that permits access to individual notes in a pre-recorded chord to fix the pitch or re-pitch that note to create a new chord. For example, you could change a piano chord from major to minor by dropping the third a half step without having to go back and re-record it. Many digital recording software packages also offer pitch correction, either through plug-in effects or simple editing procedures.

Pitch correction might be the first effect to stimulate a moral debate. For some, it represents the death of music, allowing people who can't sing or play in tune become successful stars. For others, it is merely a tool that permits perfectly fine singers and players to fix the occasional note, rather than spending hours redoing entire tracks or punching in. And for still others, it represents a new color in the palette for painting fresh sonic pictures.

WHAMMY EFFECTS

Using an expression pedal to shift a harmonized pitch up and down in real time was popularized by the invention of the DigiTech Whammy pedal in 1991. The original pedal (WH-1) will create static harmonies of a second, a minor third, a major third, a fourth, a fifth, a sixth, a seventh, or an octave above the original note, as well as a third, fourth, fifth or octave, below the note. The later Whammy II and XP-100 versions perform variations of this, with the latter throwing in wah and volume effects as well. You can blend in the additional harmony note or remove the original signal altogether, depending on the effect you seek. With its wide range of potential uses, the pedal has found fans from jazz guitarist Jim Hall to metal-monster Steve Vai.

Some use it as a sort of manual smart harmonizer, employing the expression pedal to shift the harmony from a fourth to a fifth or a major to a minor third in order to stay within the scale being played. Others dial out the original signal and use it to sweep the note from one octave to another.

As often happens in the world of effects, the original WH-1 pedal has become sought after by those who insist that it sounds better than the newer ones.

DigiTech and others have incorporated this effect in many multi-effects units. You can create it with any digital pitch-shifting device that will accept a MIDI controller and an expression pedal.

Check out the interval leaps created with a whammy effect set to jump two octaves.

The Digitech Whammy is used for various effects like static pitch shifting, interval leaps, and steel drum sounds.

CHAPTER 19
VOCODER

WHAT IS A VOCODER?

Ever since the 1970s, the sound of robotic, machine voices has spiced up pop music, television shows, and movie soundtracks, usually brought to you courtesy of the *vocoder*.

A vocoder effect combines the frequency information of one audio signal (known as the *carrier*) with the amplitude contour of a second audio signal (called the *modulator*). The modulator source usually has a distinct rhythmic character, say speech or drums, while the carrier tends to be a harmonically-rich sound such as a synthesizer string patch or pad, though an electric guitar with some grit on it can work as well.

Vocoders run both the carrier and modulator signals through

This Electro-Harmonix unit offers vocoding in a compact, inexpensive form. The "Gender Bender" control can make the sound more masculine (deeper) or feminine (higher).

banks of bandpass filters. The output level of each of the modulator's filters is analyzed and used to control the volume of the corresponding carrier signal filter. A vocoder should be inserted on the track that contains the audio material you plan to use as your modulator. The vocoder's carrier input is then set to receive signal from the track with the carrier inserted.

MODULATORS AND CARRIERS

This concept can be confusing because sometimes it is unclear exactly which is being affected: the modulator or the carrier. Let's take a simple example. To create a robot voice, you would hook up a microphone to a recording or live mixer channel. Then you would insert a vocoder, either hardware or plug-in, into this channel as an effect. This is the modulator. On another channel or track you would have a synthesizer set to a patch containing some square or saw wave information. This is the carrier and is sent to the vocoder's carrier input. Now when you play and sing, the sound of the voice will modify the notes that you play on the synth.

The vocoder may have a wet/dry control that allows some of the original vocal to come through. To check that it is set up properly, set this parameter to all wet and try singing without playing. If the routing is correct, you won't hear any vocals until you start to play.

The vocoder was developed in the 1930s as a speech coder for telecommunications applications. The name is a combination of "voice" and "encoder." Its primary use was to encrypt and transmit the voice for secure radio communication. Bell Labs engineer Homer Dudley patented the vocoder in 1938. Electronic music pioneer Bruce Haack built one of the first musical vocoders in 1969. In 1970, Wendy Carlos and Robert Moog, inspired by the vocoder designs of Homer Dudley, created a vocoder that was featured in the soundtrack to Stanley Kubrick's *A Clockwork Orange*, singing the vocal part of Beethoven's *Ninth Symphony*.

MORE THAN ROBOTS

Vocoders are not just for robotic voices. By using drums as the modulator and synth or guitar as the carrier, you can add rhythmic interest to chords played on keys or six-string, or viewed another way, harmonic content to a drum beat.

On this track, you will hear a drum modulator modulating a synth carrier, then a vocal modulating a synth, and finally the pitch tracking effect available on the Ableton Live Vocoder plug-in, which adds a fifth (of sorts) to my guitar signal.

The "talk box" effect can often be confused with that of a vocoder or Auto-Tune. A talk box is a small speaker that is connected to the output of an amplifier. The speaker output is sent through a plastic tube that is placed in the performer's mouth. By manipulating the tube with the mouth, a player can change the frequency response of the sound and add a vocal quality to the notes. The best-known example is Peter Frampton's use on *Frampton Comes Alive*, but the first recorded example was pedal-steel guitarist Pete Drake's 1964 album *Forever*.

CHAPTER 20
CHORUS

What's Ahead:

- What is chorus?
- Types of chorus
- Using chorus
- A few words about fads

WHAT IS CHORUS?

In nature, *chorus* occurs when two or more audio sources (voices, instruments, or strings on the same instrument) produce the same pitch at the same time. The name was probably derived from a typical group of voices singing together in a chorus. The effect comes from the fact that when these two distinct sources produce the same note they are rarely perfectly in tune and in time with each other. If both of these parameters were actually identical you would hear the two notes as one note. The discrepancies in time and pitch create a thicker sound than one note alone.

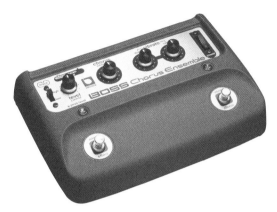

This Boss Chorus Ensemble was one of the first chorus pedals. After Boss discontinued it, it became so prized by collectors for its warm sound that the company reissued it.

TYPES OF CHORUS

As mentioned, there is natural chorus, produced by physically repeating a part, such as two guitarists playing the same part live, two voices singing in unison, parts being repeated as overdubs in the studio, the doubled strings on a twelve-string guitar or mandolin, etc. This creates the richest form of chorus sonically, but is not often reproducible live. This is where the chorus effect comes in.

The t.c. electronic chorus was popular among 1980s musicians for its high-quality sound and construction.

A chorus endeavors to reproduce the sound of doubled parts by taking a single original signal and splitting it in two. One part is sent unaltered to the output, while a second version is delayed from approximately 10 to 50 milliseconds. This emulates the natural delay between two unison parts. But that delay is not constant in nature, and what of the pitch fluctuation? As we mentioned earlier, changing a delay time can shift pitch. By using an LFO to modulate the delay time up and down, the chorus kills two birds with one stone. It varies the delay between the original and modified signals as well as varying pitch discrepancies.

Analog and digital chorus effects work slightly differently and each has its own sound. If you are going for maximum warmth and richness, go analog; if you prefer clarity and sheen, digital will work nicely.

USING CHORUS

Most choruses will have at least a depth control, which controls how much the delay changes over time, and a rate or speed control that sets the rate at which these changes take place. Some may also have a delay knob that can adjust the total delay time available, and a feedback or regeneration knob that sends the processed signal back through to be reprocessed for a more extreme effect.

Chorus can add richness to instruments and voices, but it tends to be an obvious effect, natural doubling less so than electronically emulating. It differs from pitch shifting in that it is modulated and constantly evolving rather than a static harmonic spacing. Still, its heavy-handedness can be mitigated. Here are some tips for using chorus:

- When doubling parts, you might want to think twice before tripling and quadrupling them. Sometimes a mere doubling can add more body than multiple overdubs. If you are using a chorus effect, you may want record it on a separate track and mix it in to an un-chorused track.
- There are chorus pedals available with blend knobs that add extra dry signal to the chorused signal.
- Using a compressor in front of a chorus will add to the lushness of the effect, as it keeps your signal volume up longer, giving the swirl of the chorus time be heard.
- Turning up the rate on the LFO of some choruses produces a functional Leslie sound.

On this clip, you will hear a chorus, first used for a twelve-string-type sound and then with a faster rate for a Leslie effect.

A FEW WORDS ABOUT FADS

This Electro-Harmonix Small Clone produces a sound like the one favored by Nirvana's Kurt Cobain.

In the Fuzz section, we touched on the subject of effects falling out of favor only to rise in popularity again later on. In the 1980s, chorus was all over slick pop productions. By the end of the decade, no hip band would touch it. In the 90s, Kurt Cobain's use of the Electro-Harmonix Clone Theory Chorus made the effect hip again. As of this writing, you would be hard pressed to hear it outside of current country, which is in a phase of sounding like 80s pop.

The bottom line is: If a sound inspires and stimulates you, go for it. Jazz guitar stars John Scofield, Pat Metheny, and Mike Stern have made three entirely different chorus sounds a part of their instrumental voice. If it is your sound, forget the fads—this goes for any effect in this book. Even if an effect is currently completely out of fashion, you can make it work if you use it convincingly.

CHAPTER 21
PHASING

What's Ahead:

- What is phasing?
- What is the difference between phasing and chorus?
- Using phasing

WHAT IS PHASING?

You may remember from our discussion of waveforms that sound travels in a series of peaks and valleys. A *phaser* or *phase shifter* splits the sound in two and shifts the phase of one of the signals in varying degrees of out of phase with the original. Normally, when the signals are in phase (the peak), the sound is much like the original but louder, and when the peak of one signal line up with the valley of the other (that is, out of phase), the sound all but disappears (the notch).

In a phase shifting effect, the second signal is treated with a number of all-pass filters, each with a different, extremely short delay (10-30ms) for different frequencies. An LFO alters the filter frequency ranges over time, shifting their phase through 360 degrees. This continually shifting phase creates the swooshing sound that we associate with a phaser. Most phasers employ more than one "stage," meaning that there are assorted peaks and notches taking place at different points in the time line, insuring that there is continuous amplitude available, and the signal is never phase-cancelled out of existence.

A phaser usually has a rate control to dictate how fast the phase is shifted through its cycle by the LFO, a depth control that sets how much of the altered signal is combined with the original, and sometimes a resonance or color knob that feeds the effected signal back into the effect for further processing. Some phasers allow the LFO to be synched to the song's tempo either through a tapping control or MIDI. Others might also respond to the attack envelope of the input signal, starting the phase sweep anew with each transient.

WHAT IS THE DIFFERENCE BETWEEN PHASING AND CHORUS?

Unlike chorus, phasing employs multiple static delays, as opposed to a single fluctuating delay and no pitch shifting. The sweep of the phaser affects the frequencies of the signal in a filtering fashion rather than creating a doubled sound. Though a twelve-stage phaser can sound as lush as a chorus, it presents no pitch issues when blending a part into the music. In general, phasing tends to sound more "whooshy" and less "chimey."

USING PHASING

Artists as diverse as King Crimson, Brian May, Waylon Jennings, and Eddie Van Halen have used phasing. It has been slathered on guitar, bass, drums, vocals, and even entire mixes. Any time a dream-like woosh is required, the phaser comes to the rescue. But this is not the only way to use a phaser effect. A little phasing enhanced many single note and chordal funk parts in the 1980s. Country guitar soloists discovered phasing in the 70s and it appeared on records by Merle Haggard and Emmy Lou Harris.

Extreme phasing effects can provide everything from imitation Leslie sounds to electronic madness, while subtle, slow sweeps can add motion to synthesizer and string pads.

The E-H Small Stone was one of the earliest phase shifters.

The MXR Phase 90 was used by Eddie Van Halen to add a wooshing sound to his guitar parts.

Here, a phaser is put through its paces, demonstrating rotating speaker simulation, funk envelope, and metal woosh effects. The drums are phased at the start as well.

CHAPTER 22

FLANGING

What's Ahead:

- What is flanging?
- What is the difference between flanging and chorus/phasing?
- Using flanging

WHAT IS FLANGING?

As with chorus and phasing, in a *flanging* effect the original signal is split in two. The original signal passes unaltered while the second signal is delayed by multiple delays, all in the 5-10ms (millisecond) range. The delay is constantly changed by an LFO waveform. This modulated, delayed signal is fed back on itself. This creates a lush, harmonically rich wooshing sound similar to phasing, but with more of a pitch shift.

origins

The term "flanging" comes from the way the effect was originally produced. Recording engineers would play the same signal into two tape machines while holding their thumbs on the flange on the outer edge of the tape reel. This would delay the recording on that reel of tape. When played back together, the human inconsistencies of the short delay would create a filtering effect. The resulting psychedelic woosh can be heard on Hendrix and early Small Faces records.

WHAT IS THE DIFFERENCE BETWEEN FLANGING AND CHORUS/PHASING?

A flanger can almost be thought of as a combination of a chorus and a phaser. It uses a number of modulated delays, as opposed to the single delay in a chorus or the static delays in a phaser. The modulation of the delays imparts pitch variation like a chorus, while the shorter delay time (5-10ms to the chorus' 10-50ms) creates the phaser-like sweep not heard in a chorus.

USING FLANGING

Flanging is often associated with hippie-era psychedelia, with jet plane-like swooshes serving as a metaphor for substance-induced mind-alteration, and it serves this purpose well. But flanging has much more to offer than operating as a substitute for drugs. Once you start working with its parameter controls, you will find that it is one of the more versatile effects and is as at home in a modern music environment as in a retro one.

A flanger can have a variety of controls with an assortment of names that can be confusing. The minimum controls are usually rate (sometimes called speed), and depth (sometimes called width). They may also have a delay time control (sometimes called regeneration). Some will have a "manual control" that sets the starting point or the center point of the frequency sweep. As with any effect, the best way to figure it out is to twiddle the knobs and listen to what happens. If you have downloaded the Ableton Live demo or are working with other software flangers, you may find a number of other controls like attack, release, and choices of waveform for the LFO that control the delay shift.

Some simple rules of thumb are:

- For a more metallic sounding flange, reduce the delay and increase the feedback.
- For a jet-plane woosh, turn up the feedback and depth while slowing the rate.
- Increasing the delay and rate, while lowering the depth and feedback, can serve up a chorus-like sound that was often employed by Andy Summers of the Police.
- Some software flangers allow you to synchronize the sweep to the tempo of your tracks. Using a square wave LFO and some radical parameter settings can give a drum or percussion track bell-like harmonic content.
- Some flangers will produce a decent Leslie sound at faster speeds with longish delay.

Andy Summers of The Police used an Electro-Harmonix Electric
Mistress flanger to create some of his trademark chorus sounds,
as well as psychedelic sweeps.

The drums start out flanged with the sweep matched to the tempo. Then a funk guitar lick comes in with a slight flange and the effect is removed from the drums. This is followed by a chorus-like flange on an arpeggiated part and finally a distorted guitar with a heavy sweep.

CHAPTER 23
LESLIE/ROTATOR

What's Ahead:

- What is a Leslie/Rotator effect?
- Hardware or software?
- Faking the effect

WHAT IS A LESLIE/ROTATOR EFFECT?

If you have ever heard Eric Clapton's solos on Cream's "Badge" or The Beatles' "While My Guitar Gently Weeps," Stevie Ray Vaughan's "Cold Shot," or for that matter, almost any Hammond organ ever played, you have heard the Leslie speaker effect. Originally designed for use with the organ, the Leslie has added color to guitars, pianos, and even vocals over the years.

Often contained in a wood cabinet the size of a small refrigerator, the sound of the Leslie speaker system is created by a pair of treble speaker horns pointing in opposite directions and a bass speaker pointing down. A baffle that only lets sound out through one hole surrounds the bass speaker. Only one of the treble horns is functional; the other is for balance as the pair rotates. The baffle around the bass speaker also rotates. A 40-watt tube amp that sends its signal to a passive crossover powers the speakers. This crossover splits the signal and sends high frequencies to the horn and lower frequencies to the 15" bass speaker.

The operating horn moving toward and away from your ear creates a Doppler effect. This effect is like a train blowing its horn as it approaches, passes, and moves away from you; the sound coming out of the horn seems to change pitch. This natural pitch shifting is part of what gives the Leslie its unique sound. The other parts include a kind of tremolo created by the baffle, letting the bass driver sound to pass only at certain intervals, and the distortion inherent in these powered speakers.

A player has the option of fast, slow, or no rotation, each offering a different sound. Also, due to its low-tech mechanical nature, the Leslie does not instantly go from stop to slow and slow to fast, nor does it slow down or stop immediately. Players often make use of this "ramping" up or down as a means of expression.

Though closely associated with the Hammond Organ Company, its designer, Don Leslie, began by marketing it in 1940 as the "Vibratone," built under separate auspices. It wasn't until 1980 that Hammond finally bought the name from its then owner, CBS.

HARDWARE OR SOFTWARE?

New technology and the aching backs of players have led to smaller versions of the heavy, wooden cabinet, as well as pedals, digital simulators inside of keyboards, and plug-ins that emulate everything from the Leslie's various speeds to its ramping effect. Still, those that can afford and haul one will often insist on the real thing, as this unique, acoustic-based effect is nearly impossible to completely match through mere IC chips or digital means.

FAKING THE EFFECT

If you are primarily an organist, own a van, and are on such good terms with your band mates that they are willing to help you load and unload it, a real Leslie is a thing of beauty. If you are a guitarist who occasionally does a tune that benefits from this lush sound, you will more likely be happy to approximate it.

There are a couple pedals available that are dedicated to this effect, but in a pinch, either a flanger or chorus will imply it. Set them for a fair amount of depth, not much feedback, and a fast speed. At slower speeds, these effects will sound more like what they are, flanger and chorus.

The Boss RT-20 Simulator can imitate a Leslie/Rotator effect.

CHAPTER 24
UNI-VIBE

What's Ahead:

- What is a Uni-Vibe?
- How is it different from other phasers?
- Using a Uni-Vibe effect

WHAT IS A UNI-VIBE?

Uni-Vibe is the name given by the U.S. distributor Unicord to a Japanese-designed modulation effect known in other counties as the Vibra-Chorus. Familiar to guitarists through its use by Jimi Hendrix and Robin Trower, this pedal is a type of phaser that employs transistors, four light bulbs, light cells, and an LFO to do the actual shifting. Special reflective light shields are employed to ensure the correct diffusion of light from the bulbs. Somehow, this combination conspires to create a phasing effect that is considerably more luxuriant than most pedals labeled as phasers. Chorus, vibrato, and tremolo settings are available on some Uni-Vibe-based pedals, but the classic tone associated with this pedal is the one heard on Hendrix's "The Wind Cried Mary" or Trower's "Bridge of Sighs." (See p. 115)

HOW IS IT DIFFERENT FROM OTHER PHASERS?

The use of transistors, rather than op-amps in Uni-Vibes, creates a bit of distortion that fills out the sound, making this effect sound bigger than your average phaser, which can tend to thin out the sound. Also, the four stages of filtering are set to different frequencies, adding additional richness.

USING A UNI-VIBE EFFECT

Originally designed to emulate the slow speed of a Leslie (known as the "chorale"), Uni-Vibes are rarely put to such use. The sound has become so closely associated

Dunlop manufactures a pedal that recreates the original Uni-Vibe effect.

with the late-1960s and early-70s music of Hendrix and Trower that it tends to instantly evoke an air of psychedelia. Still, the revival of the Hendrix sound by Stevie Ray Vaughan in the 80s and 90s, and Trower's continual touring have kept the 'Vibe alive. A slow Uni-Vibe can add a languid sadness to a clean sound, while the faster speeds lend a mysterious underwater whirl.

Unlike chorus or flanging, which can create equally interesting effects before or after distortion in the chain, a Uni-Vibe sound invariably works better before the breakup. Slight amp grit brings out its lushness. In addition, the Uni-Vibe sound thrives at higher gain levels, enhancing rather than muddying any overdrive that follows, making it preferable to chorus or flanging for lead work.

First a slow Uni-Vibe colors the chords, then a faster one is applied to the fills.

CHAPTER 25

RING MODULATION

What's Ahead:
- What is a ring modulator?
- What do I do with it?

WHAT IS A RING MODULATOR?

The ultimate in frequency modulation comes in the guise of the *ring modulator* effect. Rather than split the original signal into two parts, it takes the original signal and adds another one, either from an internal oscillator or an external source. The mixture produces a combination signal that is both the sum and the difference of the two frequencies.

The result is a rather random pairing of notes that, though they may be "tuned" to a key, in no way functions as a harmonizer. Rather, a ring modulator produces a dissonant, atonal, metallic series of tones that bears little relation to the signal entered. Some ring modulators include an LFO that will shift the pitch over time for even weirder sounds.

The "ring" part of the name comes from the circular layout of the four transistor diodes used to perform this process in the original processors. These were initially part of analog synthesizers and only later broken out into early units like the Electro-Harmonix Frequency Analyzer (employed to great effect by Adrian Belew).

If you lower the frequency setting of a ring modulator below audible range, it will begin to act like a tremolo unit. Conversely, if you speed some tremolos up fast enough (like the Electro-Harmonix Pulsar) they will offer a ring modulator effect.

WHAT DO I DO WITH IT?

Fortunately, most ring modulators allow some original signal to be passed through. Blending the modulated signal behind the original can add an exciting tension to solos or ostinato lines while retaining a sense of harmonic location. Adding a ring modulator to non-harmonic sounds like drums or percussion can actually add harmonic content to them, providing inspiration for compositions.

First you will hear a normal drum groove turned into a generator of two notes by using a square wave for the LFO, then a tremolo guitar part created by lowering the frequency of a ring modulator, and finally a solo part dry and then with some ring modulation in the background.

This Moog Ring Modulator offers an LFO to sweep the pitch up and down.

SECTION **5**

Delay

CHAPTER 26
TAPE DELAY

What's Ahead:

- What is tape delay?
- In the studio
- Live
- Pros and cons
- Tape delay tricks

WHAT IS TAPE DELAY?

The fact that tape delay is sometimes called tape echo helps explain the more general concept of delay. There is the familiar echo example of a mountaineer yodeling on a hilltop hearing his yodel reflected back a few seconds later, or you may have been to a concert in a large hall or stadium where you could hear the snare drum twice every time it was hit—once for the actual hit and again as it bounced off the rear wall or seats. These echoes are delayed to a greater or lesser degree depending on the distance they have to travel to and from the reflective surface. In smaller spaces, the delays are much shorter and may or may not be discerned as distinct repeats; nevertheless, they contribute to how our ears determine the size and sonic quality of a room.

In an attempt to emulate the sound of a large room or hall, early recording engineers created a loop of tape that would play back on the recording, as well as the playback heads of the tape machine. By sending a signal into this loop of tape and then varying the distance between the two heads and/or the speed of the tape, they could create a delayed signal of various lengths to blend back in with the original. By feeding the repeated signal back into the loop, they could achieve multiple repeats.

Guitarist and inventor Les Paul is generally credited with the first use of tape delay on record—as early as the late 1940s. Paul used this technique for his own records, but never marketed it to others. By the 50s, Ray Butts was building tape delay units into his EchoSonic amplifiers. These amps were favored by rockabilly legends Scotty Moore and Carl Perkins, as well as Chet Atkins.

IN THE STUDIO

Memphis producer and Elvis Presley discoverer Sam Phillips used tape echo on everything: vocals, bass, drums, guitar, etc. For this reason, the sound has become associated with early country, blues, and rockabilly, but tape echo has been a color added to a wide variety of music. The warm sound of the tape saturation, combined with the distinctive way that the continuous repeats decay, has been valued by everyone from Reggae dub producers like Lee "Scratch" Perry to Jimi Hendrix. The influence that "dub" has had on modern dance and electronica producers has made the sound of tape echo popular once again, whether produced by actual tape, hardware modelers, or plug-in emulations.

"Dub" refers to a practice of releasing a version of a track that was largely instrumental, adding extreme versions of effects like delay and reverb to the vocals, snare drum, or entire kit, as well as muting or soloing instruments.

LIVE

Once tape delay had become commonplace on recordings, the demand grew for a unit that could be used to reproduce the effect in a live situation. Stand-alone units like the Watkins Copicat in England and the enormously popular Echoplex in the U.S. soon appeared. The early, tube-powered Echoplex units are prized to this day, not just for their warm delay sound, but also for the effect that the tubes have on the original signal. Later, solid-state models are also sought after by lovers of the tape delay sound. Echoplexes varied the speed of the delay with a movable record/erase head. In the seventies, Roland released the Space Echo, which altered the speed of the tape to change the delay time, while adding chorus and reverb circuitry.

A free plug-in from the GSi company, the WatKat is a replication of the legendary British tape echo machine, the Wem Watkins "Custom" Copicat.

extras

Some early delays eschewed tape for more arcane methods of signal delay. The Tel-Ray Adineko used an oilcan, while the Italian-made Binson Echorec, favored by Pink Floyd's Dave Gilmour, employed a rotating drum.

PROS AND CONS

In the beginning, if you wanted a delay effect, tape echo was it. Once analog, and later digital delay came along, tape units began to fade from sight, at least in live performance. The new, smaller analog and digital pedals took up less stage real estate, as well as being easier to maintain. The tape in an Echoplex or Space Echo eventually suffers sonically from wear, not to mention running the risk of breakage. The magnetism from the heads gets weaker from all the knocking around during travel, and its many moving parts are subject to failure.

There are many digital delays and plug-ins out there that will give you an emulation of a tube tape echo sound, but the bottom line: Nothing quite sounds like the real deal. If that is the sound you seek, you will need to hunt a tape unit down on eBay, or buy the Fulltone Tube Tape Echo [as of this writing, they are the only ones making a new version]. Either way, be prepared to spend over a thousand dollars.

TAPE DELAY TRICKS

As is often the case, it was not long after tape delays became available that users began to abuse the effect in interesting ways.

There are many uses and cool sounds connected with delay, but tape delay excels with some of the spacier ones. By turning the feedback all the way up, you can get a runaway effect that, depending on the speed, can sound like insects or a rocket ship. Playing with the delay time while the feedback is running away creates a wealth of other psychedelic sounds that are difficult (if not impossible) to construct with analog or digital delays. The late James Gang and Deep Purple guitarist Tommy Bolin were masters at this sort of manipulation.

audio tracks 36

This clip demonstrates the sound of a tape delay as it decays and some runaway feedback effects. First, you will hear a dub-style delay on the snare drum, then the noise effects created by infinite regeneration and manipulaton of the length of the delay while it's feeding back.

danger

When using runaway feedback effects with a tape delay, or any other delay for that matter, be sure that you have quick access to your volume level or a limiter strapped across the output. "Runaway" means just what it says: the feedback will continue to regenerate over and over, and can cause the signal to get louder and louder, potentially damaging speakers or ears.

CHAPTER 27

ANALOG DELAY

What's Ahead:

- What is analog delay?
- Analog explained
- Pros and cons

WHAT IS ANALOG DELAY?

In the late 1970s, two effects companies, Electro-Harmonix and MXR, offered the first compact pedals that created a similar effect to the tape echo. These were made possible by the world-changing advent of affordable IC (integrated circuit) chips. By using these chips, a small pedal could create varying length delays and controllable amounts of feedback (sometimes called regeneration). Though analog delay times were initially relatively short (5-320ms), they were long enough to create a sort of ersatz reverb or the slap-back delays associated with rockabilly.

The Ibanez AD9's lo-fi sound helps keep repeats out of the way of the original signal.

An analog delay uses a "bucket brigade" IC chip to process the signal by passing it from stage to stage. Tapping the output at various stages offers various delayed versions of the signal. More stages mean longer delays, but the signal degrades further with each additional stage.

ANALOG EXPLAINED

In the world of recording and effects, a constant debate rages over the relative sound quality of analog versus digital. Without getting too technical, an analog process, from tape recording to analog delay, is one that deals with the original waveform of the sound and the infinite number of points along that wave.

Digital sound, on the other hand, takes the waveform and samples it at various points along the wave, converting those samples to ones and zeros. The samples are then processed before they are reconverted into a continuous wave. With the increasing power of digital processing, the sampling rate has gotten higher and higher, but while getting slightly nearer to infinite, it is still far from it. Thus, there are always those that will laud the more natural sound of the continuous curve of an analog wave.

In an analog delay, for example, at every stage of the processing it is still dealing with the full analog wave, as the sound is never converted to digital.

PROS AND CONS

Analog delays are prized for their ability to ape many of the cherished features of tape echo such as runaway feedback and signal degeneration, while providing them in a much smaller and cheaper package, without tape failure or maintenance issues. Still, die-hard tape delay fans insist that tape is worth the additional cost and problems for the distinctive sound.

The rapid signal degradation with each repeat, inherent in tape and analog delay (and even some cheap digital delays), is often considered a plus; it helps distinguish the delays from the original signal, keeping solo lines and arpeggios clear while still adding ambience. Analog delays are considered "warmer" than the digital variety, largely due to the quality of this sonic deterioration, while tape degeneration is considered warmer still.

CHAPTER 28
DIGITAL DELAY

What's Ahead:
- What is digital delay?
- Digital extras
- Pros and cons

WHAT IS DIGITAL DELAY?

A *digital delay* samples the input signal through an analog-to-digital converter, changing the samples to ones and zeros. It is then passed through a series of processors that record it into a storage buffer. This allows the stored audio to be played back in many different ways, based on parameters set by the user. The delayed ("wet") output is then sent to a digital-to-analog converter, where it is reconstituted as a continuous wave for output.

Not long after analog pedals became available, the falling price of digital signal processing (DSP) led to pricier, but still affordable digital delay rack units. Made by Lexicon, Alesis, t.c. electronic, and others, they rapidly became popular in recording studios and the racks of better-off players. As DSP costs fell further, rack units became cheaper and digital pedals arrived on the market, allowing club performers to avail themselves of the cleaner regeneration and longer delays inherent in digital processing.

The first digital delay pedal was the Boss DD-2.
Here is a more recent model, the similar DD-3.

DIGITAL EXTRAS

The processing power of digital allows these delays to offer effects not previously possible with tape or analog systems.

- Though studio engineers created the first backwards effects by flipping the tape in the studio, digital delays eventually allowed performers to take this effect to the stage by modeling the effect.

- Including a gating processing in the delay allows a "ducking" effect. This means that the level of the original signal determines the level of the delay. As the notes are played, the delay is gated down in volume or out completely, so as not to interfere with the original signal. As soon as the player or vocalist stops inputting signal, the delay comes back up, trailing off in the silence.

- Eventually, the massive amounts of processing power that could be crammed in a cheap, small package led to modeling delays like the Line 6 DL4. These units can be used to emulate the sound of tape, analog, oilcans, etc., with varying degrees of accuracy.

- Extra long delays of one second, sixteen seconds, and much more led to looping (more about this later).

The t.c. 2290 rackmount digital delay is popular for its high-quality sound, rich modulation, and ducking abilities.

The rhythm arpeggios here have a reverse delay in the background, while the lead is full on backwards.

PROS AND CONS

Digital delays produce much longer delays than tape or analog units, and the repeating notes are cleaner as they regenerate, creating near exact copies of the original. While this pristine sound is good for some things, especially in the studio, digital delay makers soon found that a high-frequency roll-off option was desirable for those who wanted to get the repeats out of the way of the original signal. Some users still prefer the unique decaying characteristics of tape and analog.

CHAPTER 29

MODULATED DELAY

What's Ahead:
- What is modulated delay?
- Using modulated delay

WHAT IS MODULATED DELAY?

Some delays offer the ability to modulate the delayed signal. At shorter delay times, these units can function as a chorus, offering a chiming, doubling effect. At longer delay times, modulation can add richness to the delay or a disconcerting waver, depending on the way the unit is set. Many delays that offer modulation will feature a rate knob to control the speed of the waver and a depth knob to determine how far sharp and flat of the original note the pitch is shifted.

First, you will hear volume swells featuring a straight digital delay and then swells where the delays have been modulated.

USING MODULATED DELAY

Wavering the pitch of delay repeats can be effective in a number of circumstances.

- As you can hear in audio track 38, volume swells become more luxurious when the delay is modulated. The trick here is to make sure that the pitch waver does not reach a nausea-inducing range of atonality.

- Often increasing the rate will allow a bit more modulation without sounding too out of tune. When using delay for doubling, some modulation can make the sound thicker, but be judicious, as it can easily turn a crisp part to mud.

- This effect can be used in place of an actual chorus. The sound tends to be less lush, but can provide an interesting and clearer alternative chime. The blend control on the delay can move it to the background for more subtle effects.

First, you will hear a regular chorus effect, then one created with a modulated delay.

The Electro-Harmonix Memory Man was one of the first analog delays to offer modulation. Bill Frisell creatively employed this capability, as did U2's The Edge.

CHAPTER 30
DELAY TIPS AND TRICKS

What's Ahead:
- Subtle uses
- Obvious uses
- Extreme uses

SUBTLE USES

There is a wide range of ways to employ tape, analog, or digital delay where the actual individual repeat or repeats will be barely discernable.

- A delay can be used when mixing a recording to create an artificial stereo doubling effect. If you are recording to tape, you will first send the signal from a single track out to a delay unit set for 10-50ms of delay, with the blend set all the way to wet and a single feedback repeat. Then, run the delayed signal back to an aux send or new channel. Panning the dry signal one way and the wet signal the other will create a stereo panning effect. The delay should be short enough that there is no audible rhythmic slap. It is here that the digital delay's inherent clarity comes into its own, creating a virtual clone of the original track. Nevertheless, analog delays can be used with the tonal variation helping to further separate the two sounds. In digital recording, it is possible to duplicate the original track, then offset the duplicate track by a few milliseconds to simulate doubling.

- A slightly longer delay (up to 250 or 300ms) can be mixed way behind a signal to extend its sustain and add a little ambience. This is especially good for single-note solo instruments and vocals. The delay should be set for a single repeat and should only be audible on extremely percussive sections—and barely even there. Panning the delay away from the original can help spread the sound across the stereo spectrum without actually doubling it. A stereo delay, with the two delays set for slightly different times, can enhance the sound further.

- Matching delay times to the tempo helps keep higher blend and/or time settings from becoming obtrusive.

OBVIOUS USES

Sometimes you wish the delay to be heard either for ambient or rhythmic purposes. For these applications, the type of delay used is important.

- The classic slapback echo heard on rockabilly vocals, guitars, bass, and drums is created with a delay time of 75-250ms, blended behind the original, but still audible. One secret to an authentic slap is to set the delay to eighth-note triplets to get the swing inherent in rockabilly music. Many modern digital delays allow you to choose a triplet setting, but if you are using a tape delay for the classic sound, or most analog models, you will have to get the groove by ear.

- A delay can turn one note into many notes in a rhythmic fashion that can create new melodies and harmonies, or percussive patterns. The Edge, from U2, is actually playing quite simple arpeggios that are multiplied by a delay set for a beat and a half of his tempo. Country pickers like Albert Lee, John Jorgenson, and Brad Paisley will use a similar setting for solos to make it sound like they are playing at twice the actual speed. This requires keeping the blend close to the volume of the original signal. Other settings, like the ones used by Brian May of Queen, can create harmonies. You need to experiment, as different delay types and different tempos will require specific settings for these effects.

- A simple drum or percussion pattern can be turned into a syncopated rhythm-fest when run through a delay set for triplets, dotted eighth notes, or quarter notes.
- Beautiful chordal pads and string or flute-style single-note lines result from long delay settings, multiple repeats, and swelling the volume of the instrument. Compressing the original signal before the volume pedal will help to enhance these swells.

On this track, you will hear a slap-back echo on both the snare drum and the guitar, creating a classic rockabilly effect.

Here, you will hear an example of how The Edge uses echo to forge his unique guitar style. First, you will hear simple arpeggios being picked, then the cascading rhythms created by adding an echo a beat and a half away. To make it even clearer, you will then hear just a single repeated note, followed by that note with delay.

EXTREME USES

Delays can be used to create wild effects that spice up any genre, but are especially useful in "dub," electronic music, experimental music, and sound design. Runaway feedback and dub-style delay on the snare were demonstrated on audio track 36 (and reverse delay on audio track 37) but here are a few more severe ways to use delay.

- Chorus-type modulation is not the only way you can add another effect to delay. Subtly flowing or extreme rhythmic filtering can add interest to a delay. When using this effect, you will want to run the filtered delay parallel with the original signal through another amp or separate mixing board channel so that the original signal remains unfiltered. Only the delayed signal is affected.

Here, a volume-swelled guitar is run through an unfiltered delay, then an auto-filter without delay, then through a delay filtered with the same auto-filter settings.

On this track, a snare drum hit is looped. First, you will hear it dry, then through a delay, followed by a filtered delay. Note how a polyrhythmic percussion track can be created out of a simple snare hit.

- Spectral delays can produce interesting results by only delaying certain frequencies of the original signal (see spectral effects in the Advanced section).
- Melvin "Wah-Wah Watson" Ragin created a signature effect by rapidly picking the high string of his guitar, mandolin style, while running his left hand up or down the neck and running through a delay set between 300ms and 500ms, with regeneration set at about 40-50 percent, and the blend at about 40 percent. Sometimes, he would do this while rocking the wah-wah pedal. Damping the string with your right hand as you pick can also have different effects.

In between a repeating, tempo-matched, delayed single note you will hear tremolo-picked notes cascading down the string with delay applied.

By using an entirely wet signal, playing with the delay times, and filtering parameters of some analog style delays or plug-in emulations, you can create experimental ambiences. These can be used for sound design or art-music projects. These can be made out of any input source, from a single guitar or keyboard note, to a percussion hit.

SECTION

6

Reverb

CHAPTER 31
NATURAL REVERB

What's Ahead:

- What is reverb?
- Parameters
- Reverb chambers

WHAT IS REVERB?

Reverb is the sound that lingers after an original sound source has stopped. When you hear a trumpet played in an open field, there is silence after the instrument leaves the player's lips. When you hear the same horn played in a large cathedral or high school gymnasium, there is a degree of decay that is heard after the last note. That sonic after-image is reverb. It differs from delay in that the sound that follows the original is not an individual, discrete, distinguishable reproduction of it, but rather a vast number of various echoes that combine to create an ambient effect.

It is no accident that churches and cathedrals are extremely reverberant. The dramatic effect has helped emphasize their spiritual nature and reinforce the power of the clergy for centuries.

Reverb can tell us many things in addition to the size of a space. The tone and quality of the reverberation can indicate the materials the space is made from, for example, a wood room will sound quite different from a concrete room. It can tell us how much damping material, like drapes or furniture is in evidence. A square room will reverberate differently than a round one.

Reverb helps us locate things in space. If you close your eyes, and a person wearing heels walks across a wood floor, you will be able to tell where they are in relation to you just by the change in the reverberation of their steps. If they speak, you can tell how near or far from you they are by the way the room's reverb affects their voice. All of these properties of reverb are important when using it as an effect, whether live or in recording situations.

This drum beat starts completely dry, is then heard in a small space, followed by a medium-size space, and finally, a large space.

As an effect, natural reverb can be considered anything that involves the use of actual space, as opposed to a reverb created by artificial means. Recording studios may have different sized rooms made of different materials, allowing instruments or vocals to be recorded with differing ambience. For example, a wood room will create a warmer sound than a concrete one. A large room with a high ceiling offers a wide variety of microphone placement options to create various types of ambience. Placing mics closer to the sound source will yield a dryer sound, while placing them further away will produce a more reverberant effect.

Sometimes, musicians or sound designers will make use of non-traditional spaces, such as a stairwell or a tiled bathroom. Each space has its own character. Just as some concert halls have been prized over the years for the musicality of their reverb, some studios offer rooms that are coveted for the ambience in which they couch the music.

Most live music is heard in a relatively reverberant space like a stadium, concert hall, or large club. Most recorded music is ultimately heard in a relatively dead space like a carpeted, furnished room, or more frequently in recent times, earphones; a completely dead space. Reverb can be used to restore some of the ambience of a live music experience. It can also be used in an artificial manner; recording material in a dead space lets a producer use hardware and software reverb to place different parts of the music in different ambient spaces to help the listener distinguish the parts, or to create an effect.

PARAMETERS

Whether dealing with real or manufactured reverb, there are certain parameters that make up the sound of a specific ambient effect.

- Reverb Time: Sometimes known as "decay" or "tail," this is the amount of time it takes the sound to decay 60 decibels from the time the original sound is cut off.
- Early Reflections: These are the first echoes that you hear off the walls and ceiling of the space, before the more diffuse decay tail. These can be more like discrete echoes.
- Predelay: This is the amount of time before you hear the first early reflection, and can have great influence on how large you perceive the size of the room to be. From 1 to 25 milliseconds is a natural predelay.
- Damping: A hard-surfaced room, say one made of stone, will produce a brighter-sounding reverb than a softer wood, or one with blankets or curtains on the wall. A control on a device or plug-in that makes the virtual surface softer is called "damping."
- Diffusion: This can reference a number of things. One relates to how close the reflections occur. Farther apart is less diffusion, and may sound more like individual echoes. More diffusion indicates repeats that are closer together. Another may be the nature of the surface off which the sound waves bounce, i.e., a rough surface will diffuse the signal more than a smooth one.
- Equalization: The decay of a reverb will vary according to the frequency.

In 1890, Harvard University professor Wallace Clement Sabine devised a formula for determining the reverb time of a room. This formula stated that the time it would take a sound to decay by 60 decibels was equal to a portion of the volume of the room divided by the sound absorption of the material in the room. This formula is used in acoustics to this day.

REVERB CHAMBERS

Reverb may be created by a natural space like a concert hall, a church, or a "live" room in a recording studio. Often, recording studio rooms (especially ones in older studios) tend to be "dead." That means the walls, floor, and ceiling are designed to absorb most of the sound rather than reflect it. This is due to the nature of multi-track recording, in which a dead space can aid in the separation of each track. A dead space insures that mistakes can be fixed later without cutting off the room decay of neighboring instruments. It also aids in matching the sound of overdubs to the original rhythm tracks. Reverb of varying types and degree is usually added later to all the tracks.

In the days before reverb hardware and software, engineers found that ambience could be added to a dead room by constructing an artificial space in which a speaker and a microphone were placed. Sound that was mic'd in the dead recording room was then sent to a speaker at one end of an artificial chamber, where the microphone at the opposite end picked it up. By adjusting the distance between the speaker and the mic, various types of reverberation were created. Once picked up by the chamber microphone, the reverberant sound was sent to its own track to be blended in with the original dry sound.

This type of space or "chamber" is still occasionally used, sometimes created from naturally occurring areas like stairwells or tiled bathrooms. Though, for example, you might not be able to fit a drum kit or guitar amp stack in these spaces, you can record their sound in an adequately sized dry room, then send it to a speaker placed on the stairs or in the tub. Concrete water tanks and large pipes have also been used to create an artificial ambience.

Sometimes reverb chambers are specifically constructed for that purpose. To avoid having to make them enormous, highly reflective material like plaster, concrete, stone, or tile is often used. The surface is made irregular to increase diffusion. These spaces tend to color the sound, which has come to be viewed as a plus. Engineers go to great lengths to match the right speakers and microphones with the surface of the chamber to create a musical coloration. The microphone should not point directly into the speaker as the idea is to pick up reverberation diffused off the chamber's walls rather than the direct signal being sent from the original track.

Some artificial chambers have become legendary. One of the first was built for Abbey Road studios in 1931—long before the Beatles recorded there. Capitol Studios, in Los Angeles, features echo chambers created from concrete bunkers built 30 feet underground. Recording artist, guitarist and inventor Les Paul helped design them as trapezoidal rooms with 10"-thick concrete walls and foot-thick concrete ceilings. These chambers were employed by music legends like Duane Eddy, Frank Sinatra, and the Beach Boys.

CHAPTER 32

SPRING REVERB

What's Ahead:

- What is a spring reverb?
- Advantages and disadvantages

WHAT IS A SPRING REVERB?

Spring Reverb uses a combination of electromagnetic and mechanical elements to emulate ambient sound. An amplifier sends the dry audio signal through an input transducer coil, which is like a tiny speaker. The movement of the coil applies a twisting force to tiny, cylindrical magnets attached to stainless steel springs. The twisting motion travels the length of

This Fender Spring Reverb unit is a reissue of the original outboard reverb offered for use with early Fender amps.

the springs and is then sent back by the output transducer, which delays the output signal.

The transducers contain damper discs; their friction creates a "braking" action on the twisting springs. The decay time of a reverb unit depends on the material type and thickness of the damper disc. Since the spring is driven with a sustained audio signal, the delayed reflections overlap the incoming sound. A single spring would produce a very one-dimensional sound, so two or three spring delay paths are used, each with a different delay-time rating. More springs result in a smoother reverb sound. This reverberated sound is then blended in with the original signal.

origins

When people began purchasing Hammond organs for their living rooms in the 1930s, they were expecting the sound that they associated with organs playing in reverberant spaces like churches and theaters. To recreate that large sound, the Hammond Company used a device created by Bell Labs to simulate the delay in long distance halls. This device employed springs and was four feet tall. Further refinement by Hammond employee and part time musician Alan Young reduced the size until it was suitable to be marketed as the Hammond Type 4 spring reverb. One of the purchasers was Leo Fender, who installed it into his Twin Reverb guitar amplifier.

ADVANTAGES AND DISADVANTAGES

Spring reverb has a distinctive lo-fi sound that is rife with historical and musical associations. Surf music is the first thing that usually comes to mind, but early reggae producers were also fond of its dark, bouncy sound. Today's roots musicians often play vintage amplifiers that come with spring reverbs installed. Others seek out stand-alone units that, whether vintage or current, go for large sums of money. They consider a spring sound to be warmer than digital reverb. Some of the most die-hard proponents of spring reverb admit that they use a minimal amount, as anything more tends to be the province of a small sub-culture of surf guitarists.

One disadvantage of spring units is that when subjected to sharp movement, they can create an atonal crash. The spring reverb of amps placed on bouncy stages can sometimes be rendered unusable due to enthusiastic drumming or band members leaping about. Another disadvantage is the fragility of the wires connecting the springs to the transducers in some units. Jarring motions, while being transported, can often result in breakage. Another consideration is that spring reverbs tend to produce a very limited frequency response, and only a fraction of the reflections produced in a real room.

Nevertheless, springs have been making a comeback as studio engineers search for "new" sounds. A spring reverb on an instrument can help set it apart in the mix while adding a mysterious darkness to its timbre. The sound is still popular enough that many digital pedals and plug-ins offer a spring reverb option.

Among its reverb types, the Electro-Harmonix Cathedral
digital reverb offers a model of the Accutronics reverb tank
used in most amps offering spring reverb.

Here is an example of a spring reverb in subtle and obvious amounts, first none, then subtle, then obvious.

CHAPTER 33
PLATE REVERB

What's Ahead:
- What is a plate reverb?
- Advantages and disadvantages

WHAT IS A PLATE REVERB?

A *plate reverb* operates much like a spring reverb, but instead of the transducer exciting vibrations in springs, it does so in a thin metal sheet, called a "plate." Two small microphones pick up the multiple reflections from the plate's edge (for stereo). The plate is mounted to a frame with springs that suspend it in mid-air so that it may oscillate freely. The frame, plate, transducer, and pickups are placed in a sound and vibration-proof box to remove interference from other sound sources. Some models have a motorized felt pad to dampen vibrations in the plate, enabling adjustment of reverb times.

The plate may be thin, but it tends to be heavy; the most famous plate reverb, the EMT 140, sports a plate that weighs in at 600 pounds; at eight feet long and four feet wide, it's not what you would call compact, either.

ADVANTAGES AND DISADVANTAGES

The plate reverb offers a much smoother, richer, and more complex reverb than a spring unit. Unfortunately, since sound travels much faster in metal than in air, the plate has to be extremely large to provide a realistic room delay. Though smaller than a dedicated chamber, they are still considered too large for most modern studios. The resonant character of a metal plate lends a brightness to this kind of reverb, albeit one that can be adjusted with equalization.

You might still find a plate reverb in some studios as a luxury, indicating that they have the room and money to own one, and as true analog processors they are coveted by those who eschew all things digital. In this age of microprocessing, plate reverbs have largely been replaced by digital reverbs, yet their distinctive sound is such that many digital hardware reverbs and plug-ins have settings that simulate a plate reverb.

The t.c. electronic Nova Reverb digital pedal not only offers an emulation of a plate reverb, but a choice of the materials from which the plate is constructed.

First you will hear the riff played without reverb, then with a smaller-sized plate, then with a bigger one.

CHAPTER 34
DIGITAL REVERB

What's Ahead:

- What is a digital reverb?
- Delay-based digital reverb
- Convolution-based digital reverb
- Advantages and disadvantages

WHAT IS DIGITAL REVERB?

Earlier, we discussed the difference between digital and analog, and how an infinite amount of analog information has to be recreated in ones and zeros. To reconstruct a reverb sound in the digital domain requires a vast amount of number crunching. It wasn't until about thirty years ago that technology reached a point where this was possible.

Early digital reverbs were hard-pressed to match the quality of a good plate when it came to realistic sound, but today they are among the most commonly used effects in the studio. The miniaturization and greater economy of processing has also made digital reverb available to the live musician. Early digital reverbs were the size of a lectern and cost $10,000, while modern ones can be as small as a pack of cigarettes and cost under $100.00.

DELAY-BASED REVERB

There are essentially two approaches to creating digital reverb: delay-based and convolution. The first is like an extremely complex digital delay, using multiple delays and feedback to build up a dense series of echoes that die out over time. You can get a good idea of how this works by taking a digital or analog delay, setting it for a short delay (10-30ms), and a feedback setting of about 50 percent. Mixed behind the original signal, this can provide something resembling reverb. A digital reverb adds delays of different sizes to increase the echo density and get closer to reverberation.

In your delay experiment, you may notice that some short delays cause a comb filtering or flanging-type of effect. Digital reverbs avoid this by adding some inverted feedback delay to create an "all-pass" filter that smoothes out the effect. The comb and all-pass regenerating delays, combined with other elements, such as filtering in the feedback path to simulate high-frequency absorption, result in a fairly accurate simulation of a real space. By doing all of this in the digital domain, the user achieves control of virtually all of the reverb parameters and the ability to create a wide variety of real and imaginary spaces.

CONVOLUTION-BASED DIGITAL REVERB

The explosion of available processing power in the new millennium has allowed a second form of digital reverb to develop called convolution reverb. This type of reverb is based on *impulse response*.

An impulse response is the sound you hear when you go into a room and clap your hands, slap a board, shoot off a gun, explode a balloon, or create any other sort of short, sharp sound. This sound brings out all of the properties of the room's reverb: decay, diffusion, pre-delay, etc.

This is because the best impulse sounds send equal energy to all frequencies. By digitally sampling the response to the impulse, a picture of the room's reverb can be captured and then applied to other sounds.

Unlike a delay-based digital reverb, a convolution reverb does not offer a programmed parameter combination that simulates the Notre Dame Cathedral; it provides the actual sampled sound of Notre Dame, to be applied to your dry snare drum or guitar, making it sound as if it had actually been recorded in that Parisian church. Using a similar method, convolution can also be used to emulate the sound of classic, expensive, delay-based reverbs like Lexicons or Eventides.

Early convolution reverbs could only reproduce the exact sound of the sampled space. If you wanted the color and texture of the Concertgebouw in Amsterdam, but with a shorter decay time, you were out of luck. You could blend in more or less of the reverberance, but the parameters remained constant. Greater available processing power now lets you take command over many of the same parameters accessible to delay-based reverb users.

Convolution reverbs come with a limited number of impulse responses from different famous and archetypical spaces. Most units or plug-ins allow you to purchase additional impulse responses or create your own to add to your library.

ADVANTAGES AND DISADVANTAGES

As digital reverbs improved to the point where they were indistinguishable by all but the most experienced professional ears from real-room sounds, they became the most widely used source of ambience in the studio. As these cycles tend to go, there followed something of a return to using actual ambient spaces for recording, but the advent of home recording and sample-based electronic and dance music has kept digital reverbs in the forefront (for most purposes). In live situations, they may be used to add ambience to a dead room and/or to split a mono signal into stereo.

Despite the geometric increase of processing power, to some ears, delay-based digital reverbs still lack the character of a real space, and though convolution versions get closer, they too fall short. Some eschew artificial reverb all together, preferring to go with miking that emphasizes the space in which the recording is taking place and using subtle delay to place instruments in the mix.

CHAPTER 35

REVERB TIPS AND TRICKS

What's Ahead:

- More or less?
- The emotion of reverb
- Mixing
- Extreme reverb tricks

MORE OR LESS?

The wash of a great-sounding reverb can be a beautiful thing. As we will discuss in the next section, it is a very evocative effect. Still, there are a number of reasons that it should be used judiciously.

In live situations, it is important to consider the reverberant properties of the room in which the performance is taking place. This would seem to be obvious, but a number of times I have witnessed instrumentalists or sound technicians slathering on the digital or spring reverb, despite the fact that they were in a room that is already extremely "live." The result is a reduction in the clarity and audibility of the performance.

Guitarists may be set up close to their amplifiers, and thus, are unaware of the effect that the room's reflections have on their sound out in the audience. What explains a similar mistake by the live sound engineers, who sometimes lay a thick layer of reverb on the vocals and/or drums in an already-ringing gymnasium or concert hall? I have no idea, but it happens. In a live room, let the actual space do the work of adding space to your sound.

Conversely, in a dead, dry room you may need to add more reverb than you think. Once again, players on stage are closer to their equipment than the audience; what may sound like plenty of reverb to them might easily get lost in the collective sound of the band and the distance to the front row. In this case, if the amp is mic'd, it is best to set the reverb for stage comfort and have the sound technician add any extra for proper sound in the house. The basic rule of thumb is to add just enough to get the job done. As to what the "job" is, we will cover that in the following sections.

THE EMOTION OF REVERB

The dark moodiness of Daniel Lanois, the bright shiny surfaces of Beyonce, the huge wash of early Def Leppard or late Country music, and the intimacy of a Paul Simon record all use reverb to help enhance the emotion they are trying to communicate. Reverb can help convey mystery, confinement, power, raucousness, joy, and more. It can sometimes express more than one feeling in the same song. It can also place a song in a particular time frame, referring to that era in an ironic or sincerely retro fashion.

Using a large amount of glossy reverb for a confessional song will undercut the closeness that is established in the lyrics. Using a vintage spring reverb on a pop vocal seeking Top 40 radio play is equally ill advised. The right tool for the right job is a fundamental tenet of reverb use.

- Spring reverbs will work well for surf, rockabilly, reggae, or retro-50s pop and soul. Some producers use it creatively in more modern applications, usually along with other reverbs.

- Plate reverbs evoke the slick pop hits of the 1970s, whether using the real deal or a digital simulation.
- Chambers, real or virtual, recall the pop hits of the 60s from groups like the Beach Boys and The Beatles. Home-built models can liven up lo-fi Indie records or experimental music.
- Digital reverbs can emulate all of the above, in addition to providing lush spaces like those identified with the jazz label ECM, and haunting atmospheres favored by Brian Eno. Basically, most modern digital reverbs can conjure up any space you need for any mood, from subtle, barely there, to cavernous pits.
- Real rooms, large or small, can give music a live feel or be used in an artificial fashion. If all the tracks are placed in the same size space, it can create the impression of musicians playing together live. If you record in, or use different real spaces and mix them together, it creates an artificial effect that can be very dramatic (i.e., drums in a small, live room mixed with strings in a concert hall space).

First, you will hear a guitar lick played with no reverb; then in order: with a room, spring, plate, and cathedral settings on a digital reverb. Listen to how the added ambience, or lack thereof, affects the emotional impact of the music.

MIXING

The types of reverb employed and the way reverb is used in producing a record can make or break the mix. In today's world of recording, most individual performances are recorded onto separate tracks—whether or not the musicians are playing at the same time or overdubbing their parts over the course of days, weeks, months, or even years. Once the tracks have all been recorded, they must be "mixed," that is to say, balanced together to create a single musical statement.

The use of reverb is essential to this process. You can use reverb in the mix to pull sounds together, separate them, or a combination of both. If all the parts were recorded simultaneously, live, in a great sounding room, there is little need for additional reverb. The sound of the instruments melding in the live space should, if mic'd properly, produce a pleasing ambience for the recording. Once you start recording things separately—even just a lead vocal that is overdubbed—the application of a reverb effect becomes crucial.

You must decide how "natural" you want your recording to sound. Placing all the parts in the same size space will result in a natural sound, but natural is not always good. We have all seen performances in a room where the bass boomed, the cymbals washed out, and the singer sounded like they were down a well because the room acoustics were too live for some of the sounds. Conversely, some dry rooms can cause the instruments to sound as if they are each playing alone, with no sense of cohesion to the sound. And, different sounds cause reverb to act differently. The sharp attack of a drumstick on the rim of a snare will create more obvious reverb decay than the soft attack of strings.

In order to be able to tailor the reverb amount to the instrument (and in the case of software reverbs, to save CPU), reverb effects are usually put on auxiliary tracks to which dry signals can be sent in differing amounts, then returned to the mix.

On this track, you will hear a drum part. First, it will be completely dry, then with a little bit sent to the reverb channel, and then with more sent to the reverb. No changes are made to the actual reverb effect. Note too, how the snare sounds more reverberant than the bass drum due to its sharper and higher pitched attack.

If you want to place all the tracks in the same space, you can do so by adding varying degrees of the same reverb to each instrument. But one of the great things about recorded sound is that it can sound significantly "better" than natural. By setting up two or more reverbs, each with its own send and return, you can tailor the sound of the reverb to the part. Even if you were going for an essentially natural sound, this would allow you to use a short decay on the reverb to which you send highly percussive sounds, while using a long decay on the reverb affecting strings and/ or keyboard pads. Mixing different types of reverb like chamber, room, spring, hall, plate, etc., can help place sounds in similar frequency ranges in their own space, thus helping to distinguish them from one another, for example, placing the vocals in a small room and the electric guitars in a larger one.

On this track, you will hear the drums and strings dry at first, then the strings with a large reverb, then a small amount of that same large reverb added to the drums. Finally, the large reverb will be removed from the drums and a smaller room reverb from a different reverb effect added. Note how the drums sound more of a piece with the strings when the same ambience is applied (or none is applied to either), and separate from the strings when the different reverb is applied.

Proper mixing involves setting up a soundstage where tracks are placed in the foreground or background, and placed, in varying degrees to the left, right or center (a really great mixer can imply a sense of up and down as well). Reverb can be a great help, or, improperly used, a hindrance in this placement.

Placing sounds in the foreground or background is largely a matter of reverb size and/or amount. Smaller spaces and/or less reverb will place a sonic object in the foreground, while more reverb and/or a larger space will set it back in the mix.

In terms of left, right, and center, it gets more complicated. A stereo reverb tends to spread the sound across the stereo spectrum. This may be exactly the effect you want as it can make vocals, drums, and guitars larger, and fill the audio picture with lush pads. But sometimes, you want to pinpoint a particular sound in space, yet still have some ambience around it. Some reverbs have a control that can either turn them fully mono, or at least bring in the width of the stereo effect.

If you do use separate and varied reverbs for each track, it is often a good idea to send all the tracks to one shared stereo reverb to help them meld.

Equalization can greatly influence the efficacy of the reverb effect on a mix. Most modern reverbs include high and low roll-off options. When using vintage springs, plates, or chambers, the judicious application of EQ before or after the reverb can help avoid muddy mixes. Cutting highs from the reverb can act in the same way as rolling off treble on a delay, allowing you to add more without getting in the way of the original signal. Also, some sound sources tend to cause high-end sizzle with some reverbs; rolling off highs from the reverb can reduce this unpleasant artifact.

Check out how rolling the low end off of the drum reverb adds clarity to the kick drum. The first two bars are with normal bass and the second two are with the bass rolled off of the reverb. The process is repeated on bars three and four.

EXTREME REVERB TRICKS

Usually, reverb amounts range from a little air added to the tracks to a grandiose, large hall-sound that imbues a sense of importance—real or overblown—to the music. Sometimes, however, reverb can be used in a dramatic but entirely unrealistic way.

- Gated Reverb: Breathes there a music fan from the 1980s with a soul so dead that they were unmoved the first time they heard the drum entrance on the Phil Collins single, "In the Air Tonight?" The power of that sound derives directly from the use of gating on the decay of the snare's reverb. The drums were recorded in a large room, giving them a huge sound. To avoid dissipating the groove in the rumble of the low end and the wash of the cymbals, the room mics were gated by the close snare drum mic so as to pass the room sound only when the snare drum hit.

First, you will hear the dry drum track, then the drums with a large, ungated reverb, then the track with the gate engaged. To eliminate any triggering of the reverb with ghost notes from the drum kit snare, I programmed an additional drum machine snare on the second and fourth beats, then sidechained the gate to the drum machine. This provides a clear trigger on those beats.

Though many claim to have been early users of gated reverb, the extreme "Phil Collins" effect is said to have come about at a Peter Gabriel session, when engineer Hugh Padgham left on the mic that Collins was using to talk to the control room, while he was playing. The mic was in the middle of the large room and created a huge drum sound. To reign in the decay and keep the drums punchy, Padgham gated the decay of the room sound off of the snare.

The Boss RV-5 pedal not only offers digital reverb in a compact pedal, but the sound of gated reverb among its choices, a sound that was obtainable only in the studio for years.

The huge, gated sound from the 80s has come to sound dated, but gating the room or digital reverb can be used subtly to fatten the sound of an anemic snare.

- Backwards Reverb: Electronic and dance music have taken digital recording and run with it — anything goes. Reversing the decay of a reverb tail can create rhythmic and/or dramatic effects. We are talking about just reversing the reverb, not the original audio. To perform this magic, it is best to make a copy of the original track, then reverse it (easily done with digital audio) and play it through a reverb of the desired length. Record the reverb and the reversed track to another track, then reverse that track. You will now have restored the original sound to its forward state, but will have a reversed reverb.

First, you will hear a distorted guitar played dry, then the guitar played though a reverb set to a long decay and 100 percent wet. Finally, you will hear the reverb in front of the distortion.

First, you will hear a dry drum groove, then the groove reversed running through a reverb, followed by the groove restored to its original direction, but with the reverb reversed. Next, you will hear the crescendo of the reversed reverb from a cymbal crash leading into the forward crash. This is followed by the same reversed reverb with the crash itself removed, and the crescendo acting as a dramatic lead into the drum groove.

- Distorted Reverb: Standard practice would be to place a reverb effect after any distorted sound, but placing distortion after the reverb can create an interesting and ominous effect.

SECTION **7**

Advanced Effects

CHAPTER 36

CONTROL

What's Ahead:

- Controlling effects on stage
- Controlling effects in the studio

CONTROLLING EFFECTS ON STAGE

Controlling effects on stage can range from extremely simple to mind-numbingly complex. If you only use a couple of pedals and always leave them set for the same parameters, control can be as easy as stepping on the appropriate on/off switch at the appropriate time in the performance. On the other hand, if you use a multitude of effects and require different parameter settings depending on the music, things get quite a bit more complicated.

One solution is a multi-effects unit. This is a pre-manufactured combination of effects housed in a rack or pedalboard configuration. Most multi-effects units allow you to set up combinations of effects set to particular parameters that can be recalled at the touch of one footswitch. Rack units require a separate pedal system that controls the rack through MIDI.

The advantages of such a system are many. Not only can you recall combinations of effects and parameters, but often you can control multiple parameters in real time with your foot through an expression pedal. Imagine being able to change the speed of your tremolo as you play, or to gradually change the amount of distortion and the delay blend simultaneously. The presets allow you to switch your entire sound from song to song, or even among song sections with a press of a footswitch.

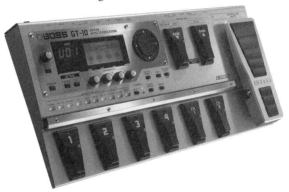

The Boss GT-10 Guitar Effects Processor contains dozens of effects, as well as extraordinary control over the parameters and combinations.

So why doesn't everyone use them? Aside from the fact that some of the more technologically-challenged musicians don't want to deal with programming and/or MIDI, for the most part, multi-effects lock you into using a single manufacturer's effects for everything. Another issue is that once programmed, it can be difficult to quickly access and change parameters if the sound is found unsuitable for that particular venue.

Lovers of character-filled standard, vintage, and boutique pedals are reluctant to give them up in the name of convenience. They are willing to do a dance, turning individual pedals on and off as needed, as well as bending over to change parameters when necessary. This also allows players to switch different brands and types of pedals in and out of the lineup at will. Multi-effects have become more sophisticated, providing loops to allow external effects pedals to be incorporated in the system, and providing quick access to important parameters.

For those with large budgets and large roadies, a compromise exists. There are MIDI systems that employ a pedal-switcher. This consists of a MIDI pedal controller and switching system. The switching system provides a number of loops (usually buffered) into which individual pedals are plugged. In addition to allowing the player to instantly access various combinations of pedals by stepping on a single footswitch of the MIDI controller, it also completely removes the pedals from the signal path when not in use, improving the overall instrument tone. The pedals are usually placed in a drawer within a rack system. This method also allows rack effects, rack multi-effects, and even amp channel switching to be included in the system and controlled along with the stompboxes.

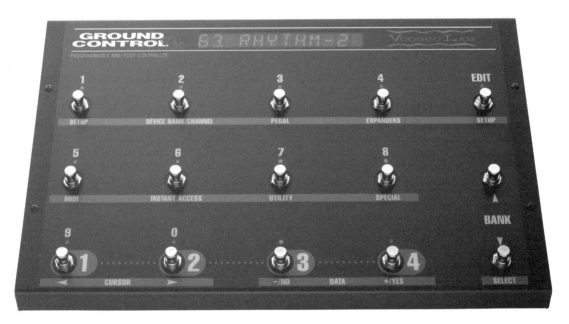

This Ground Control system allows you to plug multiple pedals into the rack-mountable GFX switcher, and then switch them in and out of your signal path with the Ground Control switcher.

A disadvantage, aside from the size of the rack and cost of the system, is that pedal parameters cannot be switched automatically. Some players get around this by employing duplicate pedals, set for different parameters.

Other players have begun to incorporate laptop computers into performance, not for backing tracks, but for effects and control. This allows them to incorporate a wealth of effects not available in pedal or multi-effect forms, like spectral and granular plug-ins (see their respective sections). It also allows effects to be easily sequenced, that is, turned on and off automatically, as well as automating parameter changes. If you play music that involves click tracks and/or live sequencing, theoretically you could never need to step on a switch through the entire performance.

Using automated plug-in sends, I placed a heavy reverb effect only on the fourth beat of the second measure of every four-measure phrase, and a long delay only on the last note of each keyboard phrase. By automating the EQ plug-in on the drums, I was able to pull out the low end (bars 5-8) or the high end (bars 13-17), for certain measures.

CONTROLLING EFFECTS IN THE STUDIO

When recording to tape using hardware effects, controlling those effects can be a complicated process. If you are comfortable committing to an effect as part of the sound, no problem. But situations that require an effect to come in and out, or even change parameters through the song, can require multiple effects with multiple effect sends and returns, complex muting operations (even more complex if the mixing board is not automated), and/or tape splicing.

With MIDI effects devices that generate and receive SMPTE and MTC time code, it becomes possible to modify effect patches and parameters as the tape rolls, and some automated boards automatically adjust effect sends and returns. This can help tape users automatically perform some of the parameter shift and mute functions available to users of DAWs and digital effects.

SMPTE is a digital timecode standard developed for film and television editing. By recording this code on a track of tape, or "striping" the tape, various devices can synchronize to the same place on the tape, making video, film, and audio editing easier. MIDI time code, or MTC, embeds the same time-locating information as SMPTE, but as a series of small "quarter-frame" MIDI messages. This allows MIDI devices like synthesizers, and digital hardware effects that can read this code, to synchronize with the tape and each other.

The digital recording age has exponentially increased the ways in which effects can be used and controlled, with plug-ins making the process infinitely easier. Any computer-based digital recording system (commonly known as Digital Audio Workstations or DAWs) can send MIDI information to hardware effects, but plug-ins are where the real fun begins. Most plug-in effects allow the majority of their parameters to be automated by the DAW being employed.

This feature of digital recording lets you, for example, easily add extra reverb to a recorded vocal on the song's chorus while radically changing the equalization of the background voices for the bridge, and adding a different delay to the outro chant.

Prior to digital recording, this would have likely required putting the verse, bridge, chorus, and outro vocals on separate tracks, or recruiting everyone in the studio for some hands-on effects controlling during the mix. With modern DAWs, each effect plug-in can be automated to do your bidding at any point in the song.

Using Ableton Live, I created a "dummy" automation clip to control both the frequency of its auto-filter plug-in effect and its on/off status, so that you hear the effect only on alternate chords. The odd "sample and hold" rhythm that you hear was created from scratch by my drawing in an automated frequency pattern. Ableton Live allows you to set up these kinds of effects and then trigger them onstage with a MIDI controller.

CHAPTER 37

MODELING

What's Ahead:

- What is modeling?
- Amp modeling software
- Amp modeling hardware
- Modeling amps
- Modeling effects
- Modeling guitars

WHAT IS MODELING?

Yet another result of cheap memory and affordable processing power is the rise of digital modeling. In one sense, digital effects like delay and reverb have always been a form of digital modeling—the attempt to recreate an analog sound in the digital domain. Digital delays were designed to create an effect that, up until that point, had been achieved with analog tape or bucket brigade chips, while digital reverbs were "modeled" after actual room sounds and spring reverbs. In more specific terms, "modeling" refers to using digital processing to mimic the particular characteristics of a particular analog device. Beginning with guitar amplifiers, modeling went on to create emulations of everything from the effects discussed in this book, to mic preamps, and even speaker responses.

The first analog devices that were widely modeled in software form were guitar amplifiers. Plentiful processing allowed software to be developed that would emulate the interaction of an amplifier's components and produce a sound reminiscent of a real tube amplifier. This software is now available as either a stand-alone plug-in or program for the computer; embedded in hardware effects; and designed into actual heads and combos. As computer power increases, the accuracy of these models approaches the real thing. It is also not unusual for producers to use modeled amplifier sounds either alone or as an adjunct to the real thing.

Still, the operative word is "approaches." Few guitarists would claim that playing through a model is exactly the same as playing through an amp, but as with many areas of modern technological life (the convenience of CDs over vinyl, and MP3s over CDs; and the convenience and economics of digital recording versus analog tape) expediency often trumps sound.

AMP MODELING SOFTWARE

Line 6's Amp Farm had the field to itself for a long time, but now, players can avail themselves of software packages like IK Multimedia's AmpliTube, Native Instruments Guitar Rig, Overloud's TH-1, Digidesign's Eleven, Waves, GTR, and Peavey's Revalver, among others. It may seem odd to consider an amplifier to be an effect, but to the extent that it is used to modify the sound of an input signal, it is, and amp modelers were very quickly pressed into service on vocals, keyboards, and drums, as well as guitars and basses.

This track starts with a guitar played through Native Instruments' Guitar Rig, used as a plug-in in Ableton Live. The opening section is a modeled Vox amplifier set relatively clean. The drums start with no effect, but after a few bars they are run through Izotope's Trash amp modeler. I removed Trash's speaker modeling and just used a little distortion from the amp (Izotope does not specify or imply particular brands). For the solo, I added Guitar Rig's simulations of a Boss compressor and Ibanez Tube Screamer, as well as their generic reverb and delay effects. The delay is synched to the tempo of the track.

Native Instruments' Guitar Rig comes with a wide variety of amp and effect models, as well as modifiers allowing the player to control the effect parameters with LFOs and instrument input level.

Modeling software offers advantages and disadvantages when recording.

Advantages

• With amp modeling software, you do not need to commit to the actual guitar sound until the final mix. What you are recording is actually an unadorned direct signal. The modeler plug-in then processes that signal. For example, should you decide at any point before the final mix that you would like the sound to be more or less distorted, or more or less trebly, you can change it. For that matter, you can decide to run it through an entirely different amp model.

• You can automate changes in the sound by automating the modeling plug-in. If you want the chorus more distorted than the verse, you can just automate the modeled amp to change at the proper point.

• Modeling gives you access to a wealth of amplifier sounds that would cost thousands of dollars to achieve with real amps—even if you rented them.

Disadvantages

• Despite the massive amounts of computing power available with the latest Macs and PCs, latency remains an issue. *Latency* is the time between when you strike the string and when the sound is produced. Running low buffer levels can reduce this to a point where it is negligible. This is fine if you are recording guitar at the very

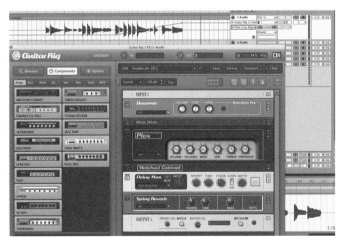

In this illustration you can see that an automation curve has been drawn raising the volume of the amplifier's Bright channel. You can also see the variety of amplifier models available.

beginning of the project, but once there are many tracks and plug-ins involved, the buffer size must be increased for the project to run, and using a software amp modeler to record a new part at that point can be problematic.

- If you take your project from one studio to another and wish to keep the sounds, you must make sure that the new studio has the same modeling software that you used.

One way around the problem of having too many instances of modeling plug-ins is to use the modeler like a real amp, recording the modeled sound through an auxiliary send to another track. This, of course, means that you can't change your mind about the sound later—just like with a real amp.

Another option would be to record all the guitar parts to two tracks, early on in the session. One track would have the modeling sound committed to the track, and one would contain just the dry, direct guitar signal. This would allow you to hear all the guitars with modeling as you are recording (just mute the direct tracks), using only one modeling instance. You could still use different sounds for each track by changing the settings on that plug-in.

Later in the session, when you are done with the guitar parts, you could add separate instances of the plug-in to the dry tracks, increasing the buffer size to handle them, and delete the tracks with the modeling committed to them. Latency would no longer be an issue because you are done playing the parts. For the mix, you could tweak each guitar track that is run through its own modeling plug-in.

With computer power increasing at a geometric rate, it won't be long before latency will no longer be an issue.

Modeling software that runs as a stand-alone program (or even a plug-in) can be used like the POD or other hardware units. Just install it on a laptop, and run out of the laptop through an audio interface into a mixing board or the interface of second computer running the recording software. This allows you to use your modeling software with minimal latency issues at any point in the project, but as with the POD, you will be committing to the sound.

AMP MODELING HARDWARE

While waiting for computer power to increase enough to allow native amp modeling plug-ins to work at all, Line 6 introduced the POD, a lima bean-shaped hardware modeler that offered latency-free recording; a number of other companies followed suit. The accessibility to a wide variety of vintage and modern amp sounds at the push of a button began to appeal to a generation of guitarists less locked into the "tubes-or-nothing" mentality.

Modeling hardware includes table top units like the Line 6 POD, as well as a plethora of rack and stomp effects, and multi-effects that include amp modeling. These devices have incorporated the modeling software into chips that are installed into the hardware. Hardware modeling comes with its own set of pros and cons.

Advantages
- With hardware, there are no compatibility issues or constant version upgrades (though firmware updates are often available).
- Latency is not an issue at any point in the recording process.
- Modeling is easily transferable from studio to studio with no authorization issues.

Disadvantages
- You must commit to a sound (unless you want to run the hardware on a bus in the patch bay).
- There are not as many options as the more high-end software like IK Multimedia's Amplitube, Native Instruments' Guitar Rig, Peavey's Revalver, etc.
- Radical revisions require buying a whole new unit.

MODELING AMPS

Modeling amps took a while to catch on, less due to sonic issues (though the early ones sounded less than stellar) than to "feel" issues. The feel problem has plagued software modelers as well. While that preset might have sounded pretty darn close to a vintage Marshall, it is only recently that modeling engineers have designed algorhythms that actually approach the complex reactive qualities of a tube amplifier.

The POD XT Pro is the rack mount version of the lima bean-shaped desktop POD that revolutionized hardware amp modeling.

There is another issue with modeling amps. Modeling software and hardware are designed to be played into a recording console and monitored through full-range studio monitors or stereo speakers. Care is taken with these products to accurately emulate different speaker cabinets and microphone placement. To send that painstaking simulation through a guitar speaker would seem to undo much of the effect that is being attempted. Only recently have modeling amplifiers begun to come with full range speakers.

Still, to the surprise of many naysayers, modeling amps have been showing up on more and more professional stages. These also have advantages and disadvantages.

Advantages
• Modeling offers solutions to preamp vs. power amp distortion/volume issues by modeling the sound of the whole amp being overdriven.
• Because they are solid state, they are cheaper, lighter, and more reliable than tube amps.
• For cover bands, they can emulate the amps of all the different acts being covered.
• For original artists, they can mimic the different amps used in the studio.

Disadvantages
• See "Hardware."
• Many modeling amps do not offer full-frequency range amplification and speakers, thus coloring the sound of the various models.

As of this writing, there are few who would maintain that a modeled Vox AC30 sounds exactly like a real, vintage AC30—especially when listening to a quality version of the real amp in a room. But mic'd up and coming through studio monitors, then matched against a variety of modeling software, professional engineers have been fooled. The feel factor is still being debated, but as computer power continues to increase, fewer guitarists are willing to discount the convenience and consistent quality of modeling.

The Vox Valvetronix models not only Vox amps, but the sounds of other manufacturers as well.

A few tips will help you make the most of your modeler:

- Many software modelers have a high-quality setting that eats up more CPU, but sounds significantly better. Be sure to use this setting for the mix even if you use the lower setting for recording.
- Don't worry about how much it sounds like the original vintage amp that it claims to model. Ask yourself, "Does it sound good?"
- Don't take the knob settings too literally. In other words, don't necessarily set them where you would on a real amp. Set them where they get you the sound you want.
- If you want the exact sound of a mic'd Marshall Plexi half-stack, buy or rent a Marshall Plexi half-stack and mic it up. Otherwise, revel in the convenience of modeling and live with the difference.

MODELING EFFECTS

Most amp modelers also include models of the standard array of guitar effects: distortions like the Ibanez TS-9 and ProCo Rat; delays like the E-H Memory Man; phasers like the MXR Phase 90, etc. These run the same gamut of accuracy and sound quality as modeled amps. Some amp modelers like Waves GTR and Digidesign's Eleven claim to work well with hardware pedals as well, but using software models offers the same advantages as software amps: automation control, recall, etc.

Once the modeling flood began, more general plug-in manufacturers began to get in the act, supplying software models of vintage recording gear such as compressors and reverbs. These are marketed to recording engineers whose ears are often more finely attuned than the most fanatic amp collector. To match the sound of beloved hardware gear requires a massive amount of processing, thus, companies like Universal Audio and t.c. electronic offer DSP (Digital Signal Processing) cards to take some of the load off of the user's computer.

The use of cards like Universal Audio's UAD card and t.c. electronic's Powercore system have the advantage of acting as security against software piracy as well. You must own the card to be able to use the software.

Despite the debate as to the accuracy of modeled effects, more and more engineers, as well as live performers, are finding that convenience overcomes the minimal difference in sound. Again, few would claim that a modeled Teletronix LA2A compressor sounds exactly like the original, but in an era where engineers are often forced to work multiple sessions at the same time, the instant recall of the exact original session settings possible with a modeled LA2A is crucial. And, as with vintage amplifiers, engineers will tell you that no two LA2As sound exactly alike to begin with, and that the latest modeled compressors are sounding just as good, if not exactly the same.

When possible, musicians and engineers are finding that a mixture of digitally modeled software and outboard analog gear presents them with the best of both worlds.

Modeling has expanded to the world of effects, with Line 6's ubiquitous DL4 delay modeler providing emulations of tape, digital, analog, reverse, and filter echo units.

MODELING GUITARS

The development of "hexaphonic" guitar pickups (a separate pickup for each string) for use with guitar synthesizers (see Chapter 38) allowed adventurous developers to take the pure signal of each string and affect it individually.

The first device to make use of this was the Roland VG-8. Because separate pitch-shift could be added to each string, this unit allowed a six-string instrument to emulate the sound of a twelve-string guitar. Individual-string pitch shifting also meant instant access to various tunings, with no intonation and buzzing problems from slackened strings.

Roland designers also began to model different guitars, allowing players to choose from single coil, humbucker, or acoustic sounds, as well as other stringed instruments like banjos and dobros. Working in the virtual realm, the software allowed guitarists to place the virtual pickups anywhere they chose along the body, or even up on the virtual neck. The current version, VG-99, references particular guitars (i.e., Telecaster, Stratocaster, or Les Paul), as well as offering modeled amps, effects, and synth sounds. Separate sounds can be assigned to different strings. For example, a synth bass sound on the 5th and 6th strings, and a nylon guitar sound on the rest. All of these sounds are modeled, not synthesized, and run directly off of the hex pickup (not thru MIDI), so there is no latency (the VG-99 does have a MIDI output to control external synthesizers).

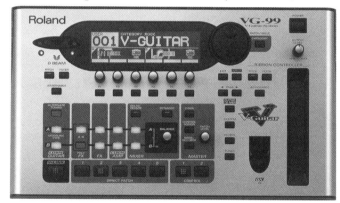

Line 6 eventually added guitar modeling to their arsenal of products with the Variax and Variax Acoustic. These instruments contain the sounds and pitch shifting onboard the guitar, and offer a more specific and wider range of instruments than the VG-99 (only instruments, no amps or effects). Separate software (Workbench) allows you to choose which instruments are available at any given time, as well as create custom instruments and tunings.

The Roland VG-99 not only models amps, but also (through the use of a hexaphonic pickup) guitars, banjos, dobros, alternate tunings, and much more.

Once again, most performers will admit, "There ain't nothin' like the real thing," but in a situation that requires a multitude of guitar sounds and tunings without the luxury of carrying multiple instruments and a roadie to handle them, many find that units like the VG-99 and Variax are a godsend.

Joni Mitchell's song catalog requires upwards of fifty-one different tunings. One of the big reasons she stopped touring in 1983 was that it had become impractical to either change tunings between every song, or carry enough guitars and hire enough techs to handle it all backstage. In 1995, Fred Walecki of L.A.'s Westwood Music built Mitchell a modified Stratocaster with a hex-pickup and introduced her to the Roland VG-8, and the problem was solved.

CHAPTER 38

CHAPTER 38
SYNTHESIZERS

> ***What's Ahead:***
> - Effects within synthesizers
> - Using effects with synthesizers
> - Guitar synthesizers
> - Synthesizers as effects/effects as synthesizers

EFFECTS WITHIN SYNTHESIZERS

Many hardware and software synthesizers include their own suite of effects like delay, reverb, chorus, ring modulation, distortion, etc. When digitally recording hardware synths, applying the onboard effects helps reduce CPU usage. With both hardware and software effects, you will often find that effect parameters can be modulated by the synthesizer's modulation matrix. In other words, you might be able to change the amount of reverb effect on the notes by how hard you play (velocity), or change the rate of the chorus by making that parameter the destination of one of the synth's LFOs.

USING EFFECTS WITH SYNTHESIZERS

As with multi-effects units, using the onboard effects of a synthesizer restricts you to the sound that the developers have chosen. However, some synthesizers do not come with onboard effects.

Whether with hardware or software, the synth player always has the option of using outboard effects. Some players like the character-filled sound that analog effects add to a digital synth.

Should you want to use effects pedals with hardware or software synths, be careful because guitar pedals are built to receive the low output instrument level signal produced by an electric guitar or bass, while hardware synthesizers and auxiliary outputs of mixing boards normally send a significantly hotter "line" level that may damage those pedals. Be sure to start with the instrument volume or send level way down.

A bit of distortion can help a synth part cut through a mix without having to raise its level. Delays can add rhythmic interest to a simple part, as well as an arpeggio effect when no appegiator is available.

On this track, you will first hear a synth part with no effect. Then, a subtle distortion will be added—just to warm it up—back to no effect for contrast, and finally, a more extreme distortion added.

First, you will hear the synth bass with a quarter-note delay to add an appegiator effect, then with a triplet delay for a funkier sound.

GUITAR SYNTHESIZERS

Are guitar synthesizers an effect? When you consider that they provide a fresh array of sounds for guitarists without requiring that they play a new instrument, guitar synths seem to fall into the effects category.

A guitar synthesizer normally consists of a hex-pickup that enables it to send separate signals from each string. Those signals are sent to a pitch-to-MIDI converter that converts the audio signal to MIDI messages. These messages allow the guitarist to play any synthesizer module, as well as send commands to switch synth or effect patches, or trigger loops. For that matter, a system could be set up to allow the performer to trigger light cues directly from the guitar strings.

The Roland GR-20 guitar synthesizer comes with a hex pickup and a floor-based module that converts the guitar string output to MIDI and triggers self-contained sounds. It also has a MIDI out to trigger other MIDI sounds and devices.

Some synth systems, like the Roland GR-20, come with everything you need: a pickup, converter, and sound module. Others like the Terratec Axon 50 or 100 are only converters, requiring external modules to create sounds.

Guitar synthesizers have been around for decades, but despite long stretches when synthesizer sounds dominated pop music, they have somehow never been adopted by significant numbers of the six-string community (bass players were even more reluctant as latency increased with the width of the string). The earliest versions did not require MIDI and were more like hexaphonic effects. These tracked very well but couldn't match actual synthesizers for sonic versatility. Still, Pat Metheny and Bill Frisell made creative use of these primitive prototypes.

The first MIDI models tracked badly, with false and dropped notes rampant, sullying the guitar synth's reputation for years. Modern versions track quite well, but still require very clean picking and damping techniques to produce accurate notes. They have found a home in some guitarist's recording studios, allowing them to add keyboard-like parts and sampled string pads without having to actually tickle the ivories. And, these parts can be easily edited and quantized for "virtually" perfect performances.

Using an Axon AX50 MIDI interface and a Graphtech Ghost system pickup, I was able to create this track in Ableton Live. I triggered Live's virtual Collision synth to create the bass line, their Analog synth for the string pad, and using the Live Arpeggiator plug-in in front of their Operator FM synth, I was able to create the tinkling chime effect by just holding down a chord and letting the arpeggiator do the rest—just like on a keyboard synth.

SYNTHESIZERS AS EFFECTS/EFFECTS AS SYNTHESIZERS

Synthesizers are not just for keyboard players. Some synthesizers like the classic Arp (and its software emulations), the Roland V-synth XT, and the Access Virus offer audio inputs that allow you to process external audio through the synthesizer's filters and LFOs. While you may not want to purchase a synth specifically for this purpose, it does allow for some sounds that are unobtainable through typical effects pedals. The more experimental pedals and plug-ins can provide some of these sounds, but running a track through a synth's processors can still create some unique effects.

This short piece of music was constructed without keyboards, pedals, or filtering plug-ins other than the Way Out Ware TimewARP virtual Arp synthesizer. All of the sounds were created by playing a guitar through Overloud's TH-1 amp modeling software and using various patches on the TimewARP. The drums were run through a synth filter as well.

Say you want synth-style sounds, but don't want to have anything to do with hex pickups or actual synthesizers, real or virtual. Using a few basic or not-so-basic effects, whether in pedal or plug-in form, you can turn your guitar, bass, or electric piano into an electronic music generator in no time. Here are some tips:

- Plug in a wah-wah pedal, but instead of using the wah in a rhythmic manner, rock it slowly, employing it like a synth filter, controlling the envelope with your foot.

- Better yet, use a synth-style filter like one of the Moogerfooger pedals or a plug-in like Ableton Live's Auto Filter. The sound is qualitatively different than a wah pedal, but either can be controlled with a pedal, just like a wah.

- Distortions and fuzz pedals work better than overdrives to create that synthesizer buzz saw effect.

- Many tremolo pedals offer choppier waveforms in addition to the standard Fender-style tremolo. Try them out for cool synth LFO effects.

- Octaver pedals create the synth effect of two oscillators an octave apart; here, an overdrive can add some grit. Be sure to place it after the octave pedal to ensure that the octaver sees a pure signal.

- Try setting a Whammy pedal for an octave up and removing the original signal. Roll off the high end to reduce artifacts and swell in with a volume knob or pedal to simulate attack delay.

The Moog MIDI MuRF can create synth-style, sequenced, analog filtering effects without having to run your instrument through a synthesizer.

CHAPTER 39
LOOPING

Looping simply means taking a piece of audio and playing it back in such a way that when it reaches the end of the recording, it starts over.

What's Ahead:
- Ambient looping
- Time-based looping
- Looping tricks and tips

Almost as soon as recording to tape was invented, people began to splice the tape into loops that would continuously repeat. But even before that, composers like Milhaud, Hindemith, Varèse, and Cage used turntables to create musical loops. Turntable and tape loop compositions often used sounds that were previously considered unmusical (machine noises, speech) to create music.

In the 1970s, Brian Eno and Robert Fripp introduced tape looping to pop music. Fripp also helped introduce the concept of "live" looping, creating loops on the spot in performance using two reel-to-reel tape recorders.

AMBIENT LOOPING

Ambient looping refers to creating loops of layered sounds that do not require synchronization with other more rhythmic elements of the composition or performance. This type of looping creates an atmosphere that can add emotional impact to a piece of music or a song. It is also used in sound design for radio, film, or television.

Ambient loops may consist of short phrases piled on top of one another, long sustained sounds layered together, or a combination of the two. The first layer of recorded sound usually determines the length of the loop, but some loopers allow you to later extend the loop time.

Looping tools have come a long way since multiple tape loops and sound-on-sound recording tape echo units. Modern digital loopers like the Line 6 DL4, the Boomerang Phrase sample, the Oberheim Echoplex, and the granddaddy of digital loopers, the Electro-Harmonix 16-Second delay, allow you to speed up, slow down, and reverse individual layers. In some cases, they also allow you to change the length of individual layers as well. In the hands of masters like Bill Frisell and David Torn, these options help create loops of astounding complexity and beauty.

Here is a loop built up with guitar parts: notes swelled in, strings scraped and plucked behind the nut, harmonics, etc. Some parts were reversed and then additional parts were added on top going forward. After that loop fades out, you will hear the same loop fade in run through bit reduction, a filter, and a resonator effect that adds pitch-like overtones.

TIME-BASED LOOPING

When the various layers of a loop contain rhythmic elements that must be synchronized, it is considered time-based looping. You might say that the entire genre of hip-hop has its origins in time-based looping. When DJs match repeating loops created with two turntables, that is time-based looping. When hip-hop producers grab a rhythmic sample and combine it with another rhythmic sample, that is also time-based looping.

As with almost everything else, the advent of digital processing has made time-based looping easier. Where 1980s DJs had to manipulate turntable motors to match audio from two records, the turntablists of the new millennium now use programs that timestretch audio to match tempos without affecting the pitch of the source. Programs like Ableton Live and Garageband are based around this digital wizardry, allowing you to grab various audio loops — bass, drum, vocals — and have them line up in perfect rhythm.

Here, we have a picking part that has been looped and an additional part added. Next, the part is reversed. Then, another similar loop has been slowed to half-speed, at which time I placed a picking part on top; when returned to normal speed, you hear the second part at double-time and an octave higher (this was a technique commonly used by early looper Les Paul). This second loop is then reversed as well.

LOOPING TRICKS AND TIPS

Successful looping requires talent and practice. Here are some tips to help you get started:

The Boss RC20-XL Phrase Recorder Loop Station has an Auto Start feature that starts automatically, recording only after the unit detects an audio signal.

- When attempting time-based looping in a live situation, setting accurate start and stop points for the initial loop can be tricky. Hardware users may need to become familiar with the response of the unit's footswitches. Some hardware loopers offer quantization, where they will be more forgiving of rushed or dragged switch implementation. Others can be synched by MIDI to drum machines or sequencers.

- With ambient loops, it is important that the end and the beginning flow smoothly into one another. One way to insure this is to set a loop length by starting and stopping the recording process without playing anything, and then go into overdub mode (some loopers will automatically do this when you exit the record mode). This allows you to enter audio across the start/end point of the loop without any clicks or pops.

- Reversing, slowing, or speeding up the recorded material, then adding other sounds will add interest. Returning the original audio to forward and/or its original speed will then modify the second layer of looping.

- Other effects may be added either pre- or post-looping. That is, you may want to run your signal through a reverb for one layer, a filter for the next, and distortion for the third. After the loop is recorded, running it through delays, reverbs, distortions, or any of the full panoply of available effects can create an entirely different atmosphere than that evoked by the original loop.

CHAPTER 40

GRANULAR EFFECTS

What's Ahead:
- What is granular audio?
- Granular effects

WHAT IS GRANULAR AUDIO?

Granular audio is the process of dividing audio into extremely short snippets (or "grains"). We are talking about lengths of 1–50 milliseconds; at these lengths, the sound is no longer identifiable as the original source, becoming more of an atmosphere or glitch.

First, you will hear the audio source (in this case a French horn sample) and then you will hear it divided into tiny grains, with small spaces in between.

GRANULAR EFFECTS

Granular effects manipulate those sections. These treatments include varying the speed, phase volume, and pitch. Sometimes, delays are used to move sections forward and back in time.

Here is the same French horn with the pitch and frequencies of the various grains shifted.

You can create your own granular effects by taking an audio clip and putting it in a sampler, then adjusting the start and end points of the sample to a tiny section of audio. Using a MIDI controller or MIDI automation, you can shift the sample start point to create an ever-evolving tonality.

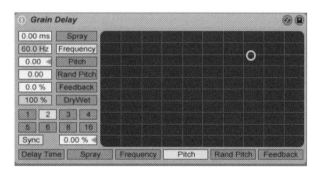

This Ableton Live Grain Delay plug-in separates
the audio signal into grains and then manipulates
the delay and pitch.

CHAPTER 41
SPECTRAL EFFECTS

What's Ahead:

- What does spectral mean?
- Spectral delay
- Spectral distortion

WHAT DOES SPECTRAL MEAN?

When the term *spectral* is applied to effects, it refers to the fact that the effect is applied differently to different frequency bands of the audio material. You may remember the term "multiband compression" from the earlier chapter on compression; it referred to compression being applied only to certain frequency ranges of a signal, for example, compressing just the low end of a mix while leaving the mids and highs uncompressed. A similar process can be applied to other effects as well.

SPECTRAL DELAY

Spectral delays allow you to delay a particular frequency range of a signal while leaving the rest of the spectrum dry. This can prove useful when working with a full drum-kit loop, where you might want to create a more complex rhythm by adding delays to the snare and high-hat, but leave the bass drum alone to avoid muddying up the works.

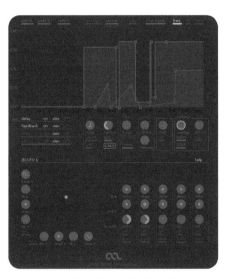

You could also set a long delay, with near infinite repeats, for the low-end strings of a guitar to create a sort of bass loop, and then solo over that on the more moderately affected high stings.

A spectral delay plug-in (Artificial Audio's Obelisk) has been applied to only the mid and upper frequencies of this drum loop. Note how the bass drum remains unaffected while the snare and cymbals are delayed with a dotted-eighth note delay. Note too, how when the original's audio is shut off, the delays tail off differently for different frequency ranges.

Artificial Audio's Obelisk plug-in allows you to delay specific frequency ranges of the audio sent through it.

SPECTRAL DISTORTION

In similar fashion, a spectral distortion effect will allow you to apply different amounts and types of distortion to different parts of the frequency spectrum. Once again, when dealing with a drum loop, you may want to keep the low end dirt-free, but add some grit to the snare mid-range and/or just a little sizzle to the cymbals.

Guitarists may want their mid-range to roar while the low end merely crunches, avoiding conflict with the bass and bass drum. Spectral distortion effects allow you to fine tune the amount of distortion at each frequency.

Using Izotope's Trash plug-in, I am able to apply three different types and amounts of distortion to the frequency spectrum of a drum loop. Here, you will hear the frequency ranges shift and the resulting change in the character of the lows, mids, and highs. There is no equalization change taking place, just amounts of distortion on various frequencies.

Songs

Walking on the Moon: The Police

LEGEND

Drummer: Stewart Copeland

The Police were inspired as much by the production and arranging of reggae as by the songs. Delay was a common effect on reggae records—and not restricted to guitar and/or vocals. On this track, the hi-hat is put through a delay to create a distinctive rhythmic part, while the reverb on the snare drum is delayed as well. On the breakdown after the first chorus, you can hear the snare side stick through the delay, adding to the song's mystery.

Walking on the Moon

Music and Lyrics by Sting

audio tracks 68

Intro
Reggae feel ♩ = 147

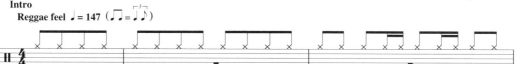

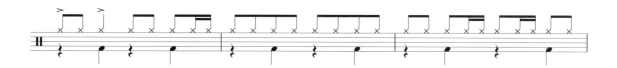

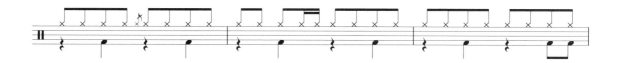

© 1979 G.M. SUMNER
Administered by EMI MUSIC PUBLISHING LIMITED
All Rights Reserved   International Copyright Secured   Used by Permission

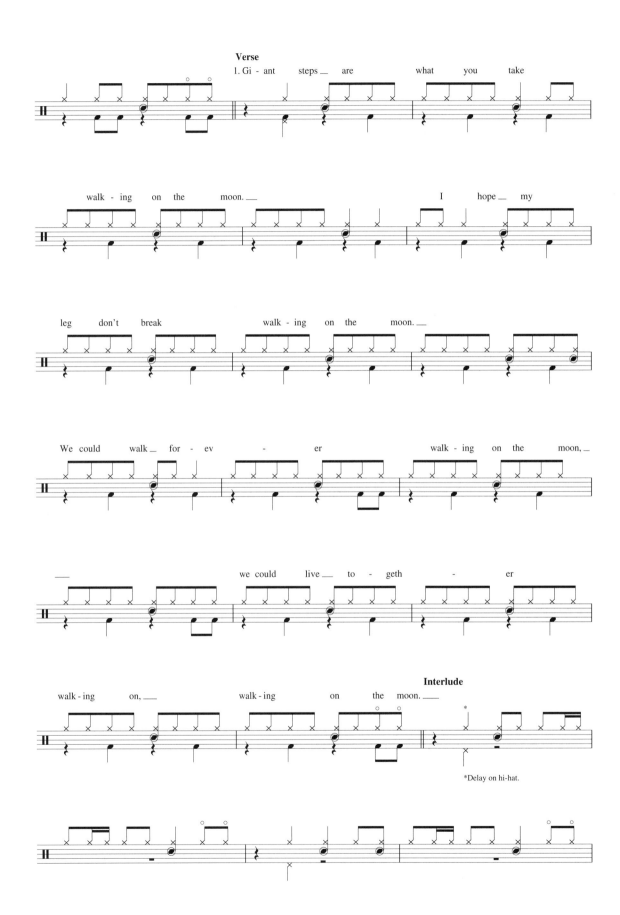

*Delay on hi-hat.

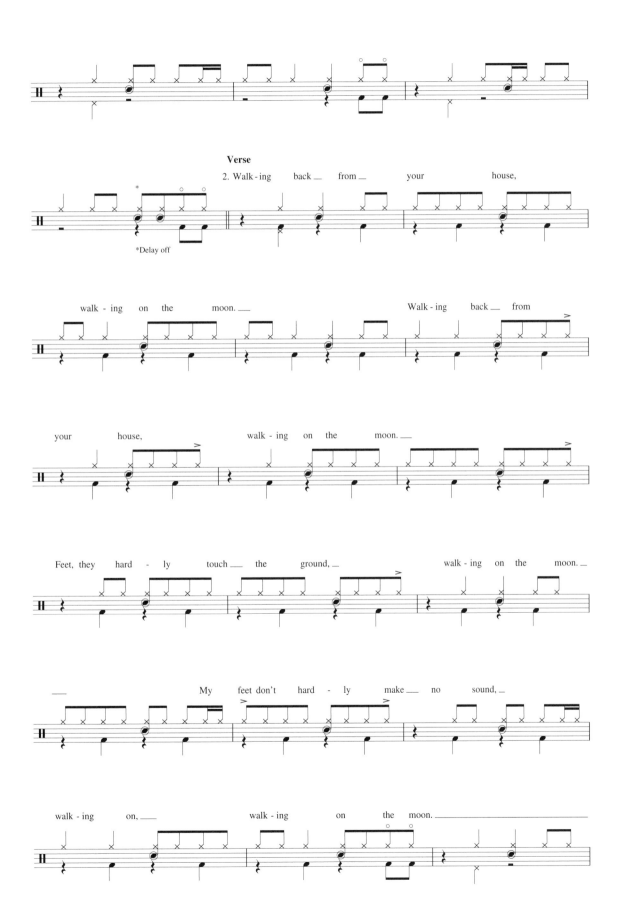

Verse

2. Walk - ing back __ from __ your house,

*Delay off

walk - ing on the moon. __   Walk - ing back __ from

your house,   walk - ing on the moon. __

Feet, they hard - ly touch __ the ground, __   walk - ing on the moon. __

__ My feet don't hard - ly make __ no sound, __

walk - ing on, __   walk - ing on the moon. _____

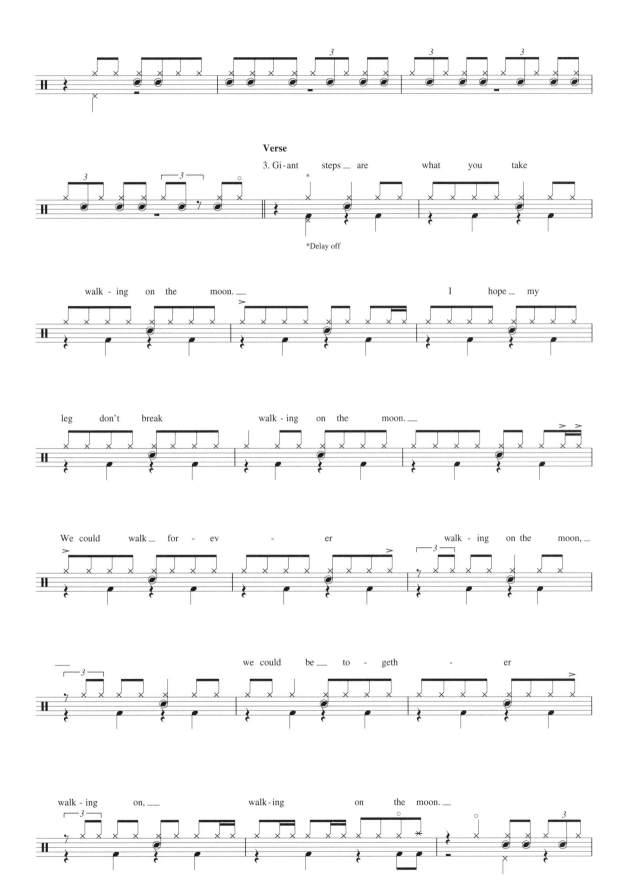

Verse

3. Gi-ant   steps _ are   what   you   take

*Delay off

walk-ing   on the   moon. _   I   hope _ my

leg   don't   break   walk-ing   on the   moon. _

We could   walk _ for - ev -   er   walk-ing   on the   moon, _

_   we could   be _ to - geth -   er

walk-ing   on, _   walk-ing   on   the   moon. _

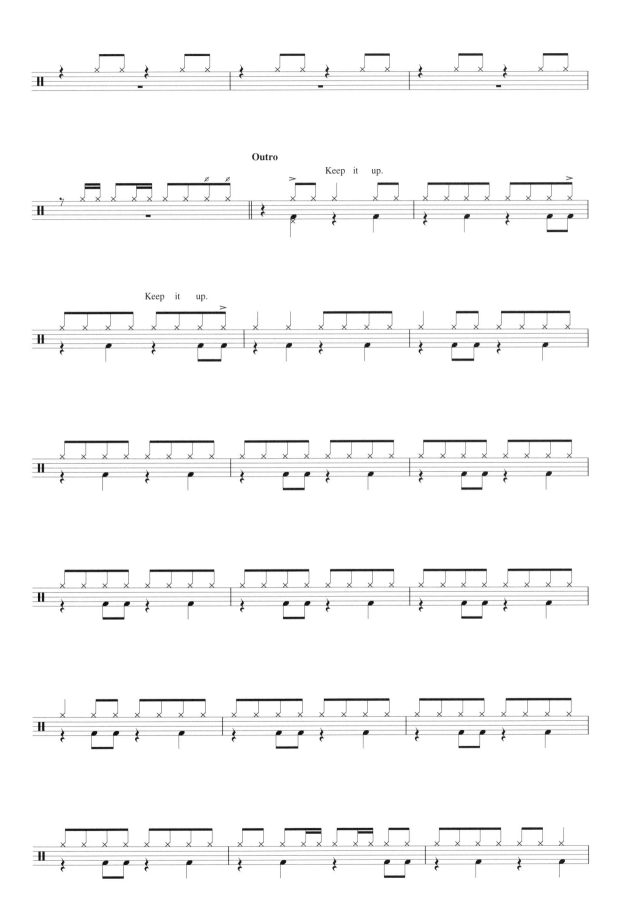

*Delay off

Begin fade

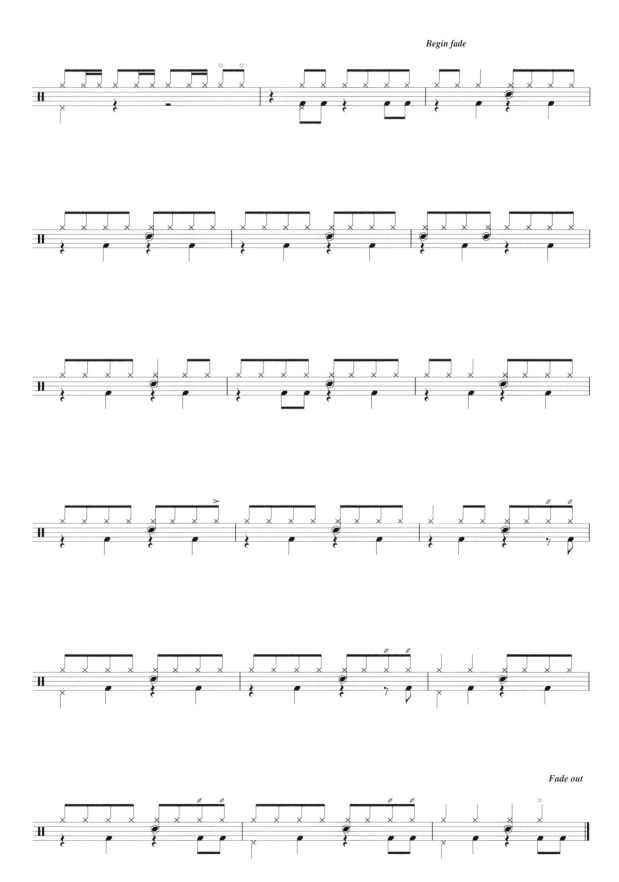

Fade out

Bridge of Sighs: Robin Trower

Robin Trower has suffered from comparisons to Jimi Hendrix, and though he has admittedly been heavily influenced by the American guitar genius, this Brit has developed a signature sound that is instantly identifiable as his own. For one thing, while Hendrix occasionally used the then-new Uni-Vibe effect, Trower has made it an integral part of his instrumental voice. Its breathy, slow sweep here beautifully recalls the sighs of the tune's title.

Bridge of Sighs

Words and Music by Robin Trower

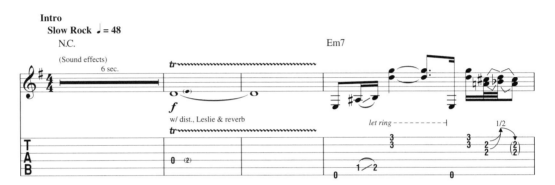

Copyright © 1974 Chrysalis Music Ltd.
Copyright Renewed
All Rights for the U.S. and Canada Administered by Chrysalis Music
All Rights Reserved   Used by Permission

Owner of a Lonely Heart: Yes

Trevor Rabin contributed an intro containing two flavors of distorted power chords, as well as funky and sweeping flanged picking parts to this hit. Still, it is for his fabulous harmonized solo that he is remembered. Rabin used an MXR Pitch Transposer to achieve a sound that echoed producer/keyboardist Trevor Horn's orchestral work on a solo that was itself beautifully orchestrated, previewing Rabin's future as a scorer of films.

Owner of a Lonely Heart

Words and Music by Trevor Horn, Jon Anderson,
Trevor Rabin and Chris Squire

Copyright © 1983 by Carlin Music Corp., Unforgettable Songs and Affirmative Music
All Rights for Carlin Music Corp. in the U.S. and Canada Administered by Carbert Music Inc.
All Rights for Affirmative Music Administered by Warner-Tamerlane Publishing Corp.
International Copyright Secured   All Rights Reserved

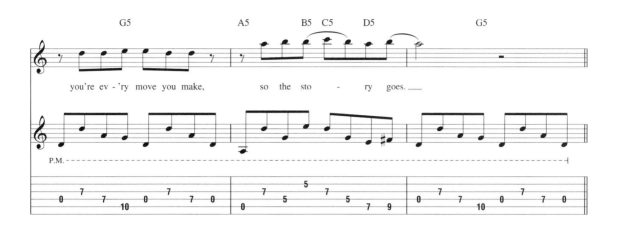

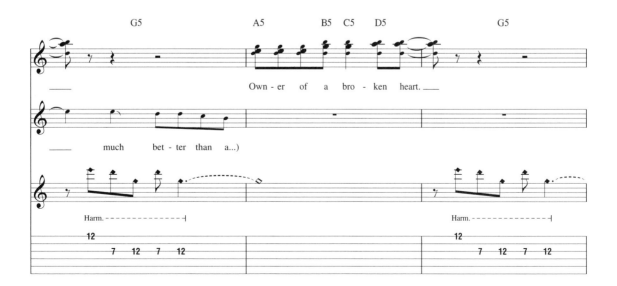

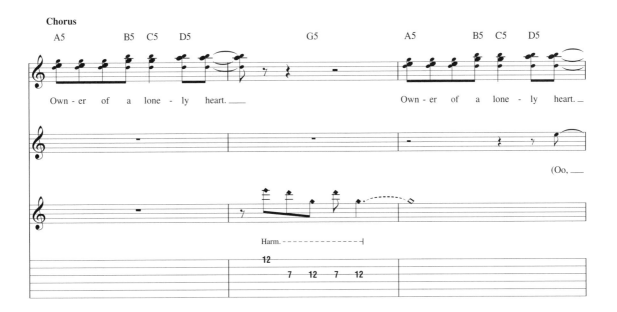

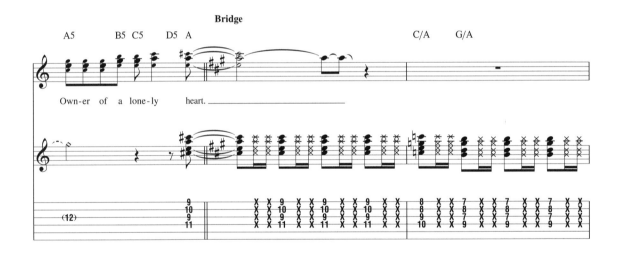

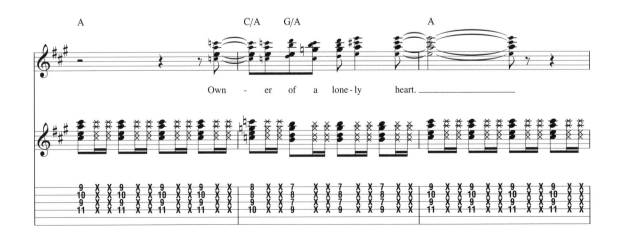

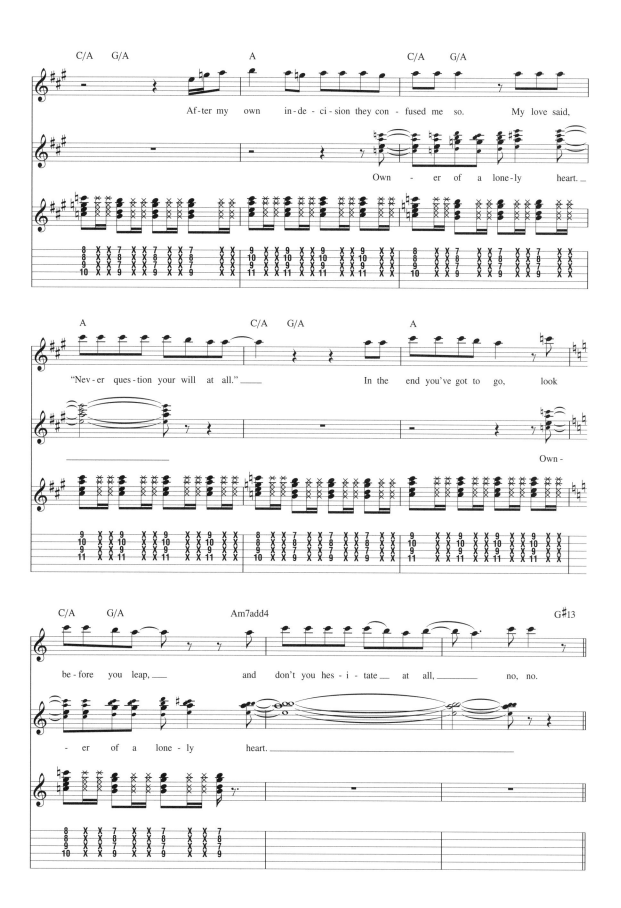

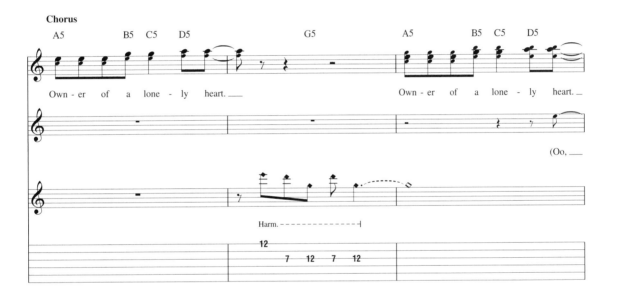

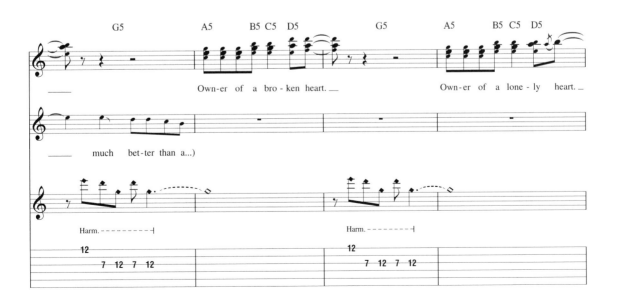

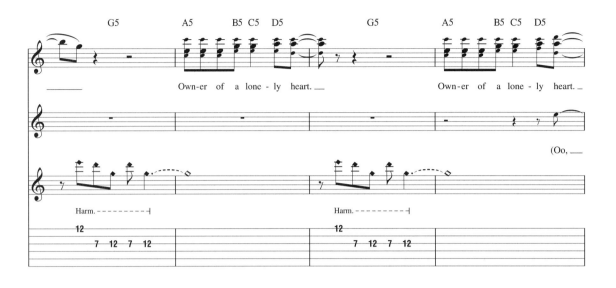

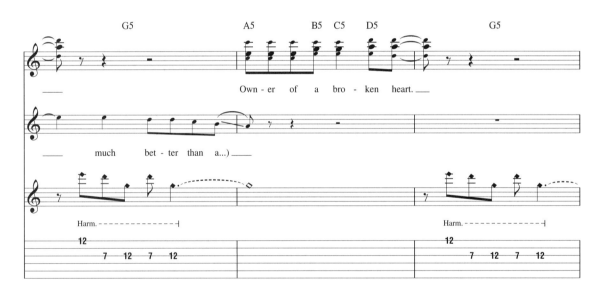

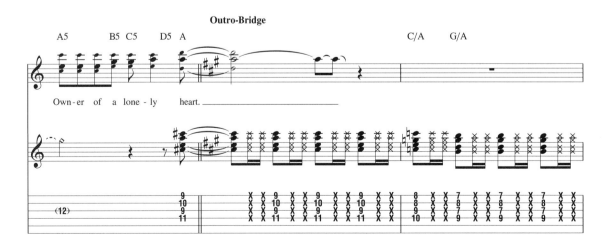

Eruption: Van Halen

Like Michael Jordan and Joe Montana, Eddie Van Halen transcends the boundaries of his chosen field. Whether or not you are a fan of heavy metal, his genius is undeniable. This talent exploded on the scene in part through the aptly named "Eruption." His unique application of two-handed tapping and penchant for combining classical, blues, and rock elements created a truly new and exciting sound. As "heavy" as his music is, if you listen closely to this and other Van Halen tunes—especially the early ones—you will note that while his tone is distorted, it exhibits but a fraction of the gain employed by many of the guitarists that he influenced.

Eruption

Music by David Lee Roth, Edward Van Halen,
Alex Van Halen and Michael Anthony

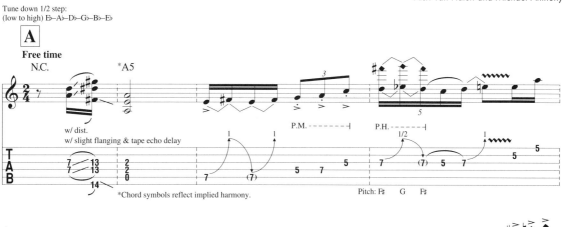

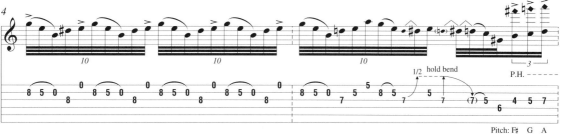

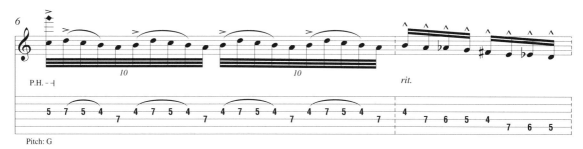

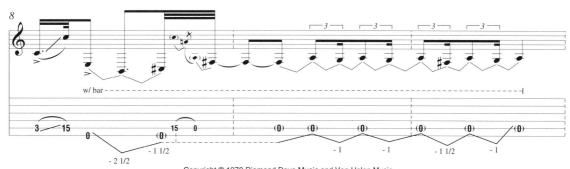

Copyright © 1978 Diamond Dave Music and Van Halen Music
All Rights for Diamond Dave Music Administered by Red Stripe Plane Music, LLC
All Rights for Van Halen Music Administered by WB Music Corp.
All Rights Reserved   Used by Permission

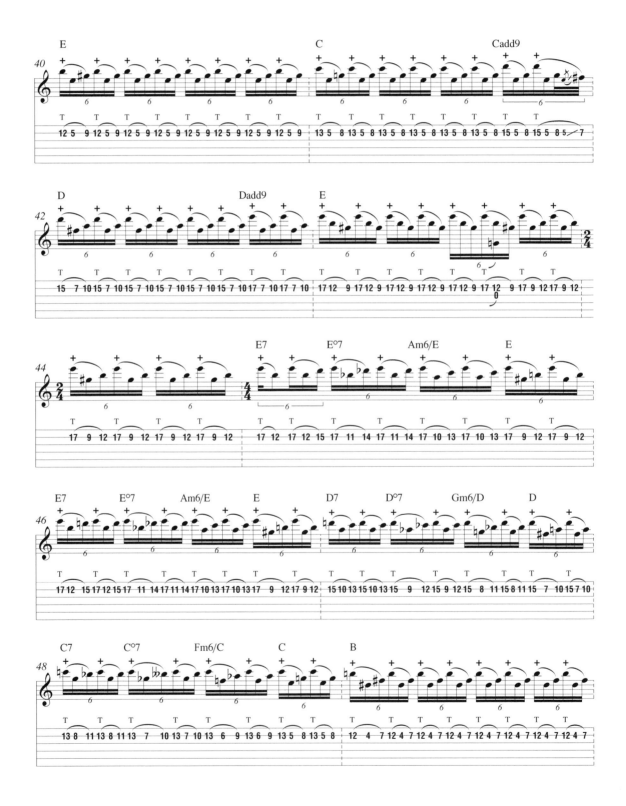

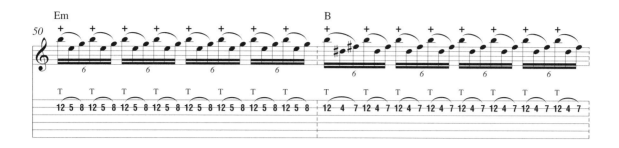

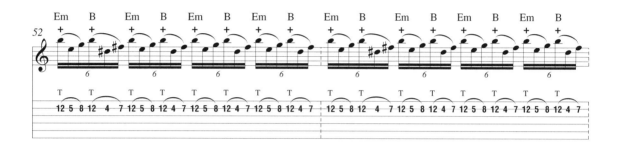

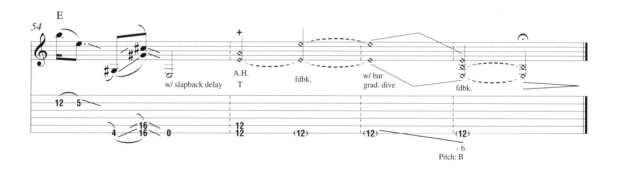

Pipeline: The Chantays

In surfer parlance, a "pipeline" is the curl of a big wave. A talented surfer will tuck him or herself under this curl and ride within it to the shore. Surf music's love of reverb may be because its tubular sound serves as a metaphor for the tubular shape of the curl. On this classic surf instrumental, you can hear the reverb best on the mandolin descent down the low string at the beginning and the hard-attacked rhythm picking throughout. Using reverb for these parts, instead of delay, prevents the rhythm from being affected while providing plenty of ambience.

Pipeline

By Bob Spickard and Brian Carman

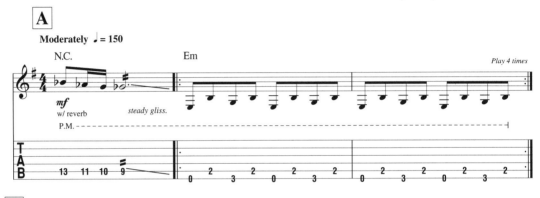

Copyright © 1962, 1963 (Renewed) by Regent Music Corporation (BMI)
International Copyright Secured   All Rights Reserved
Used by Permission

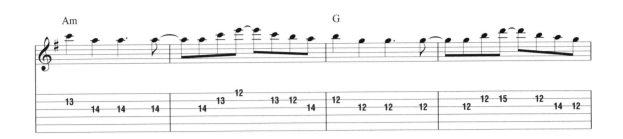

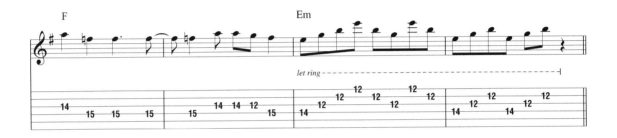

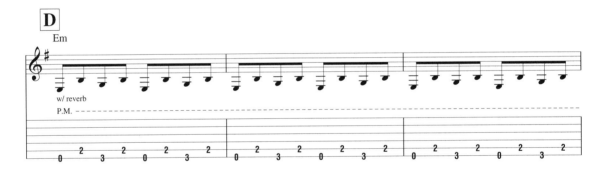

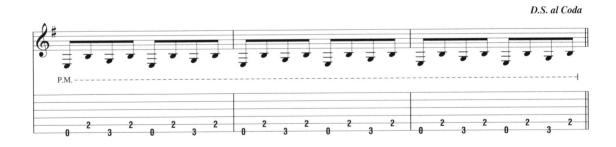

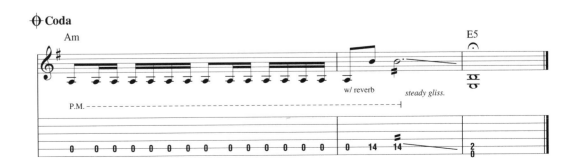

APPENDIX

PEDAL TIPS

Probably the most often asked question by musicians entering the endless world of pedal acquisition and usage is, "In what order do the pedals go?" As with anything concerning sound production, the answer is fairly subjective and mutable. Still, there is a starting point that will help you understand how the signal chain works. Once you understand that, feel free to experiment with putting pedals in the "wrong" position. You might come up with something you like!

The following list is in order from the instrument to the amplifier. In the case of a series of plug-ins, the order is from the input to the output, but the positioning is even more flexible.

• Vintage fuzz pedals, and/or auto-filters (or auto-wahs): As was discussed in the fuzz chapter, vintage units work best with direct input from a guitar. Auto-filters respond directly to the dynamics of the instrument, so you don't want anything in front of them reducing those dynamics. Using both a fuzz and auto-filter together is not optimal, but is possible with the fuzz coming first. If you want a distorted auto-wah sound, you are better off using a standard distortion pedal after the filter.

• Compressors: In the absence of fuzz or auto-wahs, this will come first in the chain as it increases the noise level of any effects that come before it. You do not want to use a compressor in front of an envelope-filter as it will reduce the dynamic range and limit the effect of the filter. Compression will enhance any ambient effects that come after it.

• Wah-wah pedals: These can actually come before or after a compressor, and though most often used before distortion or overdrive pedals (but not fuzz), they can come after. Try both, and see which sound you like.

• Distortion and/or overdrive pedals: These pedals like to see a clean, dynamic signal, so they should come early in the chain, before any modulation devices. One trick is to use a moderate level of gain on the distortion device and activate a compressor placed in front of it to enhance sustain without muddying the sound with tons of grit.

• Modulation pedals: Tremolo, chorus, and/or flanging are usually next. These pedals are purposely messing with your instrument signal—splitting it, wavering it—and thus, are not ideally placed in front of your overdrive. If you are using the amplifier's preamp for your distortion, these effects, along with those that follow, are best placed in the amp's effects loop, as it comes after the preamp stage. If you are using full-on power amp distortion, you may want to consider splitting your guitar signal so that a dry sound goes into your distorted amp with the effects going into a separate amp or amps.

• Delay: This effect normally comes next, just before the final effect—reverb. Sometimes, however, adding an effect like an auto-filter, flanger, or chorus after the delay can make interesting sounds.

• Reverb: This tends to be the last effect in the chain, though as I mentioned in the reverb chapter, for radical sounds, adding effects after the reverb can be interesting.

The second most-common question is, "Which is the best overdrive/chorus/tremolo/delay/ etc.?" Understandably, musicians who are new to the world of pedals, and many old hands as well, want to narrow their search for a delay pedal by asking more experienced players, "What should I get? Which is the best one?" This is a valid question, but unanswerable. I touched on this dilemma in the introduction. Other musicians can let you know what is available that they have used and liked, but in the current climate where thousands of different pedals are available, the concept of "best" is most assuredly moot.

That said, I recommend that you check out trade magazines like *Guitar Player, Guitar World, Premier Guitar, Keyboard, Bass Player, Mix, EQ, Electronic Musician,* as well as the British versions of these magazines (or whichever ones are still in print or online by the time you read this). Check out a manufacturer's website to watch videos or listen to sound clips. I suggest that you avoid chat rooms, message boards, and amateur YouTube clips. Though everyone is entitled to their opinion, you are likely to be steered better by professionals than hobbyists. Unfortunately, an amateur YouTube clip by a less-than-stellar player can make a great effect sound awful.

It is true that there are great players out there who are not professionals, but by checking out the rigs and recommendations of musicians who play night after night, you are more likely to get accurate information about a pedal's abilities and drawbacks. By reading about the pedalboards of musicians already getting the sound that you seek, you will at least find a starting point for your purchases.

POWER

Hardware effects require power to keep them running, whether that means batteries, onboard power supplies and a power cable, or wall-wart adapters. Batteries can work fine for pedals like compressors, filters, and distortions. Modulation and ambient devices, like chorus and delays, tend to use up batteries very quickly. Some players don't like to deal with adapters or power supplies, and will use only batteries. If you number among these, be sure to put fresh batteries in your modulation and delay devices before each gig. Alkaline batteries are recommended, as they last longer than the cheaper zinc-carbon style.

Some effects that respond better to zinc-carbon batteries are rare exceptions to the alkaline rule. This will be stipulated in their manual.

Because distortions, overdrives, and compressors last so long on a single battery, it is easy to forget to replace them regularly. Unfortunately, the pedals do not necessarily go from working well to not at all. In some pedals, they just start to sound different (some players actually prefer the sound of some overdrives with weakened batteries, leading to power supplies that emulate this voltage reduction). More often, they start to sound bad very gradually, which can create extreme frustration before you realize that the problem is just a dying battery.

There are a variety of power supplies available for pedals. Some pedals come with a wall-wart or recommend specific optional adapters sold by the manufacturing company. When you start to accumulate pedals for your stage show, all these adapters can become unwieldy.

The truth is that a single adapter can often power a number of pedals. Boss offered one of the first multi-pedal power supplies with their PSM-5. The Godlyke PA-9 and Visual Sound's 1 Spot are also single adapters that will power a multitude of pedals. Powering all your pedals with this type of multiple-pedal power supply can sometimes work, but while they are small and inexpensive, they can also generate unpredictable transients and extraneous noise. And, there are pedals like the Line 6 Modelers and Boss Twin pedals that require high current and will not work with this type of adapter.

This may be why the Voodoo Lab Pedal Power 2 Plus has come to be nearly ubiquitous on pedalboards and in racks. It features isolated outputs for each pedal to prevent line noise, and will power Line 6 and Boss Twin Pedals. It features an output that will emulate dying batteries for extra sag on some overdrives, and offers a standard AC outlet for any pedals not covered. It is also short-circuit protected, meaning that if you have a short in a power cable, or a pedal malfunctions, it will temporarily turn off the power to that pedal, while other outputs continue to function normally.

Always check the polarity of the pedal before using any adapter. Most pedals are positive ring, negative tip, but if you use that kind of adapter with a pedal that is the opposite polarity, you risk permanently damaging the pedal.

PEDALBOARDS

Pedalboards can run the gamut from a piece of plywood with a couple of pedals attached, to a massive, metal behemoth with 15-20 pedals arranged in rows and levels. What you need will be determined by the kind of gigs you play and the number of pedals you use. Many musicians have multiple boards in different sizes and configurations for different gigs, for example, a small board with a few pedals for local dates; a slightly larger one in a bag that will fit in the overhead, or a small flight case for fly-dates; and a mega-board for touring. Whichever kind you construct, there are a few things to keep in mind.

- Cable companies like George L's and Planet Waves make kits that allow you to construct cables of any length. These will help you customize the lengths to fit your needs. Keeping cable lengths to a minimum will help reduce capacitance that sucks high end from your sound.
- Velcro should be industrial strength. Make sure the bottom of the pedal is clean before attaching the Velcro.
- While Velcro will make it easier to try out different pedals, it won't always keep the pedals attached when constantly transporting the board. For boards that will see a lot of travel time, cable ties are a better bet. You can drill holes through a wooden board, or string them around the bars that make up the metal boards offered by Pedaltrain.
- Before you purchase a board with a built-in power supply, make sure that it will power your particular pedals.
- Lay out all your pedals on the floor in such a way that they are easily accessible to your foot for switching, and figure out if you need to construct multiple levels before attaching anything. Pedaltrain and a company called Stagetrix offer individual pedal risers that make accessing pedals in the back row of your board much simpler.

EFFECTS RECOMMENDATIONS

As I have mentioned a number of times, the notion of which effects are best, or better than others, is highly subjective. Also, manufacturers come and go, instantly dating this kind of information. That said, if you are reading this book, you are obviously seeking guidance in all things relating to effects. I would feel remiss if I let you wander through the maze of available sonic modifiers without offering some recommendations of specific products, based on years of experience employing effects on stage, in the studio, and reviewing them for major guitar magazines. Thanks to eBay, effects that are no longer produced are still available to the happy hunter.

I have broken this information down according to the same subdivisions as the sections and chapters in the book, suggesting products based on what they do well. This will allow you to extrapolate what it is that you need for the sound you want, hopefully saving countless hours and thousands of dollars weeding through the morass of effect options out there. I have avoided getting into the vintage voodoo syndrome as much as possible; these are mostly great-sounding, available pedals that won't strain your budget. Most of them have been around for years because they do the job well. Once you start here and get used to the sound of each effect, there is plenty of time to go in search of the perfect version. I have generally listed pedals, with the occasional outstanding studio rack unit or plug-in thrown in.

The same manufacturers come up often, so the websites are listed separately (in alphabetical order).

VOLUME PEDALS

Boss FV50H or FV50L
If you are looking for lightweight and reliable, these plastic babies can't be beat. The "H" is for high-impedance input (like a guitar), and the "L" is for low-impedance (like keyboards).

Ernie Ball
If you are less concerned with weight and more concerned with sound and taper, try the metal Ernie Ball line.

TREMOLO

Danelectro Tuna Melt
This cheap, tiny pedal may require an eBay search, and if you find some, buy two, as they are not sturdy (though mine has lasted years). Still, for the money they sound great and fit in a gig bag with room for a book.

Cusack Tap-A-Whirl
On the other end of the spectrum, this pedal sounds great, offers all the bells and whistles (tap-tempo, ramp up and down, multiple wave forms), and is built like a tank.

SoundToys Tremolator
This plug-in combines the usual great SoundToys tone with the ability to synch the tempo to your project, adjust the accent, control the amount of swing or shuffle, and design your own staggered rhythms.

COMPRESSION

MXR Dyna Comp
This simple pedal is the sound of country guitar circa 1980-90, and was employed by Adrian Belew in the early King Crimson days to make his rhythms pop and his leads sustain forever—not transparent, but basic and awesome.

Keeley Compressor
This has taken off as the guitar tone guru's compressor of choice. It is cleaner and quieter than the Dyna Comp (and much more expensive).

Visual Comp 66
Falling near the MXR price, but with a more transparent sound and a tone control, the Comp 66 has a slightly larger footprint than either of the others, but is a great pedal for the money.

Universal Audio/Empirical Labs
These are two names that keep coming up in articles about recording; they offer the crème-de-la-crème of outboard audio compression.

WAH WAH PEDALS

Dunlop Wahs

Your first stop in wah shopping should be the Dunlop website. They offer all the classic Cry Baby wahs, as well as fancier models with adjustable Qs and artist models that will send you straight to the sound of your favorite player. The basic Cry Baby Classic should handle your wah needs until you fine-tune exactly what you are looking for in a wah.

AUTO FILTERS

Moog

Moog's Moogerfooger pedals are the ultimate analog filter pedals: beautifully built, amazing sound, and attendant price tags. Fabulous funky filtering starts here.

Electro-Harmonix

The less expensive E-H makes a terrific range of filter effects in various sonic colors and footprint sizes at affordable prices.

SoundToys FilterFreak

When it comes to plug-ins, it is hard to beat this baby for versatility and sonic richness. It is CPU hungry, but worth it.

TAL Filter

This is the first of a number of TAL-Togu plug-ins I will recommend. This one is a filter that sounds terrific, synchs to tempo, and self-oscillates for a realistic Theremin sound. Best of all, every one of the TAL-Togu plug-ins mentioned here is FREE!

EQ

MXR EQ

For meat and potatoes pedalboard sound shaping, or for radically shifting your equalization for an effect, the MXR 6- and 10-band graphic EQ pedals are hard to beat. Built like tanks, reasonably priced, and voiced for musical instruments, they are a great place to start.

BOOSTERS

Keeley

Keeley makes the Java Boost, which is a germanium-based treble boost if you want to color your tone like the classic 60s and 70s players or the Katana Pre Amp for a more transparent boost.

65 Amps

Their British spelling, Colour Boost, is a secret weapon that offers a cool, red-chicken-head four-way knob that dials in Clapton, Page, Peter Green, Brian May, and other recognizable classic colors (or colours).

Xotic Pedals

If the American studio sound is your bag, the Xotic AC Booster, RC Booster, and BB Preamp pedals are for you. These pedals scream L.A. Session: think Mike Landau, Scott Henderson, Tim Pierce, etc.

OVERDRIVES

Ibanez TS9/808 Tube Screamer
These are the original classic overdrives from which most other ODs are derived. This doesn't mean that they are the "best," just that they have become a touchstone. The 808 was the first, and some swear by its creamy tone. The TS9 sound is a little edgier. There are a number of people doing modifications of the new models to make them sound more "vintage." The bottom line is that if you love the Stevie Ray Vaughan tone, one of these pedals, or the dozens of clones and mods, will help you get it (so will using very heavy strings, tuning down to E♭, and playing very loudly).

Hermida Zendrive
If Robben Ford's tone is more to your taste, this is the pedal. Robben himself uses it through a Fender Twin Reverb when he doesn't want to take out his Dumble amps.

Xotic AC+ and BB+
Once again, for that smooth, LA-studio sound, these twin pedals will deliver. They allow you to cascade either channel into the other and are very versatile. The AC+ is more Fender/Dumble-like, while the BB+ is more British-sounding, but both have distinctive tones of their own.

Jetter Jetdrive
Newer on the scene is a personal favorite: the Jetter Jettdrive. Like the AC+ and BB+, it has two differently voiced channels that cascade into each other. Unlike the Xotic pedals, it lends less of a sonic footprint to the sound, allowing you to carve your own.

Barge Concepts BP-1
This is another personal favorite, a little-known pedal based on the even-lesser-known Interfax HP-1 Harmonic Percolator (you can't make this stuff up). This is another dual channel pedal that runs the gamut from transparent clean boost, through mild drive, up to sick, highly compressed fuzz.

DISTORTION

Pro Co Rat
If it is good enough for Jeff Beck, John Scofield, and Bill Frisell, it might just be good enough for you. The range of sounds produced by the aforementioned artists is a great testimonial to the versatility and musicality of this simple distortion pedal.

Boss, Digitech, Zoom
Boss, Zoom, and Digitech make over a dozen different distortion pedals each. Most are available at any major music store. The truth is that many famous hard rock and heavy metal players are using high-gain amps for most of their distortion. If they do use a pedal, they seem to favor Boss distortions or overdrives in front of these already overdriven amps. The Zoom pedals and heavy metal pedals by Boss and Digitech are great for younger or amateur players who can't afford high-end high gain amplifiers (or don't play at rock club and stadium volumes). They are great for approximating the shred sound in a bedroom or garage.

FUZZ

Electro-Harmonix Big Muff
This is great for smooth, fat, sustaining fuzz ala Fripp, Mudhoney, Jack White, Smashing Pumpkins, etc. It is not really for Hendrix tone—It's not particularly dynamic or volume sensitive.

Dunlop Fuzz Face/Analog Man Sun Face
In the right hands, these children of the Dallas Arbiter Fuzz Face provide a rich, creamy fuzz sound that responds to the volume level of the guitar for a wide variety of gritty tones. Experienced touch and attack are required to bring out the best in this style fuzz.

Fender Blender
Used by Billy Corrigan of Smashing Pumpkins and Kevin Shields of My Bloody Valentine, the Fender Blender offers an upper octave overtone and a much harsher sound than the Big Muff or Fuzz Face.

One website alone offers almost 50 different fuzz pedals, so while these cover the basic flavors, there are many others from which to choose.

BIT REDUCTION

WMD Geiger Counter
This cool pedal offers bit reduction and downsampling with optional expression pedal control.

Alesis Bitrman
You will have to search eBay for this hard-to-find baby. Not exactly a foot pedal, it was originally sold as a DJ product, but offers some great bit reduction, ring modulation, and frequency shifting effects to the adventurous musician of any kind.

Tal-Bitcrusher
Another free plug-in, this one offers bit depth and downsampling, as well as white noise and EQ.

PITCH SHIFTING

Eventide H8000
The mother of all pitch shifter/harmonizers, this two-space rack unit is incredibly high quality and wildly versatile, as well as extremely expensive. Trumpeter Jon Hassell and guitarist Steve Vai swear by them (and can afford them).

Digitech Whammy
Tom Morello of Rage Against the Machine, Jonny Greenwood of Radiohead, The Edge, David Gilmour; name a guitarist whose signature is sound as much as notes and you will doubtless find a Digitech Whammy on these players' boards. Many swear by the original models, which used a different chip than the current variety, but either way, this is the pitch-pedal standard.

VOCODERS

Korg microKorg XL/R3
These two synthesizers from Korg include vocoder effects as part of their feature set.

Electro-Harmonix V256 Vocoder
E-H offers a vocoder and auto-tune pedal in its affordable tradition.

CHORUS

Boss CE-1/CH-20/CE-5/CH-1
The old, gray Boss CE-1 Chorus Vibrato pedal is a discontinued unit that is prized among chorus aficionados. The newer CH-20 twin pedal has a CE-1 setting modeling the original for those who don't want to spend eBay bucks. Either the CE-5 or the CH-1 are good solid workhorse chorus pedals with the added advantage of effect level controls that allow you to set the effect and then blend in the amount that you want.

Arion Chorus
This was a cheap pedal that was adopted by studio pros in the 1980s for its lush sound, and thus became collectable. E.W.S. offers an expensive mod that installs a 3PDT switch that makes the pedal true bypass, modifies the tone adjustment for a smoother sound, adds a vivid blue LED, and makes the chorus and vibe mode switchable.

Electro-Harmonix Clone Theory
This chorus avoids implying an 80s sound through its distinctive tone and by being associated primarily with Kurt Cobain of Nirvana. It now comes in "Small" and "Nano" sizes as well.

PHASERS

MXR Phase 90/100
The Phase 90 is a classic phasing sound used by everyone from Eddie Van Halen to country guitarists. The Phase 100 offers a choice of deeper Q voicings.

Electro-Harmonix Small Stone
Equally classic, it sounds audibly different than the Phase 90. The Color switch deepens the Q.

FLANGERS

Electro-Harmonix Deluxe Electric Mistress
Dave Gilmour and Andy Summers made this flanger famous.

MXR M-117R Flanger
The basic MXR Flanger was another pedal used on many classic recordings.

LESLIE/ROTATOR

Hughes & Kettner Tube Rotosphere
Guitarists who can afford the pedalboard space and the price prize this tube-powered pedal.

Boss RT-20
This dual pedal takes up a little less space and has a cool pulsating light.

UNI-VIBE

Fulltone mini-Deja 2/mini-Deja 'Vibe
These are favored among Uni-Vibe fanatics.

Dunlop Uni-Vibe
For the less fanatical, but still a great Vibe.

Jetter Gear Vibe
A great-sounding Vibe for those who want to save pedalboard space (no bigger than a Dyna-Comp).

RING MODULATION

Electro-Harmonix Ring Thing Sideband Modulator
This is a great, affordable, freak-out pedal.

Moog Music MF102 Moogerfooger Ring Modulator Pedal
For almost twice the price of the E-H ring modulator, this classy pedal offers wood sides, more sonic options, and more control possibilities.

TAPE DELAY

Fulltone Tube Tape Echo
If you decide to go this route you are best off just springing for this unit. A vintage piece will cost at least as much and be more prone to breakdown.

ANALOG DELAY

Electro Harmonix Memory Toy
At well under $100 this is a great place to start. Also check out E-H's Memory Boy, and legendary Deluxe Memory Man (Andy Summers, The Edge, Eric Johnson) pedals.

MXR Carbon Copy
This is another reasonably priced analog delay pedal.

Diamond Pedals Memory Lane 2, Moog Analog Delay/Maxon AD-999
At the other end of the spectrum, you have expensive boutique pedals like these, with more controls.

DIGITAL DELAY

Line 6 DL4
This digital modeling pedal has become the go-to pedal for pros, due to its accurate emulations of analog, tape, and digital delays. It also has filter delays, reverse delays, and other delay-based effects, as well as tap tempo and looping.

DigiTech TimeBender
This is a contender to unseat the DL-4 with great sounding delays and the ability to set tempo and/or rhythmic patterns by strumming a guitar silently.

Boss DD-3

This basic digital delay has been around for over 20 years, and will serve many players for another 20.

TC Electronic 2290

This rack unit was prized for its ducking ability. Production has been discontinued, but TC now manufactures the D2, which offers many similar features.

SoundToys EchoBoy

The EchoBoy is one of the best delay plug-ins out there, and offers great sound and extreme versatility.

Tal-Dub

I prefer this one to the TAL-DUB-II. It is great for dub effects, lo-fi delays, and runaway oscillation effects. Map the controls to a MIDI controller, and it virtually becomes an instrument.

SPRING REVERB

'63 Fender Tube Reverb

The real deal—if you can afford it.

RV-1 Real Spring Reverb/RVB-1 Reverbulator

Solid state, one is a rack and one is a floor model (though I can't imagine stomping on springs). They're not cheap, but are more portable than the Fender.

PLATE REVERB

Overloud BREVERB

If you want a real plate reverb, you will have to search eBay or build your own. In the interim, this plug-in does a fine job of emulating some classic plates.

DIGITAL REVERB

Hermida Reverb

For a basic reverb to add some air to an amp that doesn't come with the effect, this inexpensive pedal is hard to beat.

Boss RV5

Road-tested and offering stereo versions of various types of reverb, the RV5 is a classic workhorse.

Electro-Harmonix Holy Grail

This is priced right and now available in the smaller, yet hardier "nano" version. Many musicians swear by its sound.

Lexicon, Eventide, TC Electronic

These companies all offer classic, high-end reverb rack units for studio work. TC and Eventide now have pedal-size versions for those with pedal board real estate and a little extra cash.

CONTROLLERS

Behringer FC1010
With plenty of switches and continuous real-time control options, this widely used MIDI foot controller offers maximum parameter command for the buck.

Voodoo Lab Ground Control Pro
Another popular MIDI foot controller, this is often combined with Voodoo Lab's GCX audio switcher to switch pedals in and out of the chain.

AMP MODELING SOFTWARE

Overloud TH-1
This often-overlooked amp modeling software sounds and feels great, and is easy to use. It is not, however, as full-featured as some of the others.

Native Instruments Guitar Rig
With its synth-based effects parameter modifiers like LFO and step sequencer modules, this one is best for more adventurous sound designers, less so for vintage fans.

IK Multimedia Amplitube
This creates great-sounding amps and effects, but is not as easy to navigate as Guitar Rig.

Line 6 POD Farm
These are the guys that started it all, and the sounds are great. Lazy Susan style GUI (not the easiest to work with).

Studio Devil Amp Modeler Pro
Easy to use, low price, great sound, though more basic in features than the others.

LOOPERS

Line 6 DL4
The looping function of the DL4 is probably the most widely used hardware looper out there, offering foot control of half-speed and reverse. Also check out the more elaborate M-9 and M13 Stompbox modelers for their looping functions. Can't store loops.

Boss RC-20 Loop Station
More features than the DL4, the Loop Station stores loops, changes loop tempo without changing pitch, etc., but does not drop loops an octave by halving the speed. More advanced loopers will want to check out the RC-50 for multi-tracking capabilities.

Boomerang Phrase Sampler
Boomerang offers a larger footprint, but more full-featured looper products, i.e., multiple loop lengths and synching to other Boomerang pedals. Boomerang III offers multiple tracking like the RC-50.

Electro-Harmonix
Some loopers swear by the original E-H 16-Second Digital Delay (the reissue was not as successfully received). E-H's 2880 does multi-track looping ala the RC-50 and Boomerang III.

Gibson Echoplex Digital Pro

For serious loopers, the Echoplex was originally made by Oberheim—a synth company bought by Gibson—and allows you to insert new sections into an existing looper, offers various synching options, and much more in a single rack unit.

Looperlative

MIDI-controlled, high-end rack looper for boutique-oriented musicians.

ODDITIES

Etherwave Theremin

Technically, in the right hands, a Theremin is a musical instrument, not an effect. So few of those hands exist that for most, this sci-fi pitch producer serves more as an effect (think "Good Vibrations" or the soundtrack to the original *The Day the Earth Stood Still*). Creating different pitches as you move one hand while raising and lowering the volume with the other is not for everyone, but the new Moog version of this classic electronic device also serves as a control-voltage controller, allowing you to control parameters of other effects by waving your hands around.

Korg Kaoss Pads

These devices feature a sampler, effects, and an X/Y pad. You can run audio through them and add effects whose parameters are controlled in real time by the pad. Or, you can sample the audio and hold it in the unit while you add and control effects. Originally designed for DJs, it has since been adopted by guitarists and keyboard players to add new dimensions to their music.

MANUFACTURERS' WEBSITES

Analog Man
analogman.com

Barge Concepts
bargeconcepts.com

Boomerang Musical
Products
boomerangmusic.com

Boss
bossus.com

Cusack Pedals
cusackmusic.com

Demeter Amplification
demeteramps.com

Diamond Pedals
diamondpedals.com

Digitech
digitech.com

Electro-Harmonix
ehx.com

Ernie Ball
ernieball.com

Eventide
eventide.com

E.W.S.
ews-us.com

Fender
fender.com

Fulltone
fulltone.com

Gibson
gibson.com

Hermida Audio
hermidaaudio.com

Hughes & Kettner
hughes-and-kettner.com

Ibanez
ibanez.com

IK Multimedia
ikmultimedia.com

Jetter Gear
jettergear.com

Korg
korg.com

Line 6
line6.com

Looperlative
looperlative.com

Maxon
maxonfx.com

Moog
moogmusic.com

(MXR) Jim Dunlop
jimdunlop.com

Native Instruments
native-instruments.com

Overloud
overloud.com

Pro Co
procosound.com

Robert Keeley
robertkeeley.com

SoundToys
soundtoys.com

TAL Togu Audio Line
kunz.corrupt.ch

TC Electronic
tcelectronic.com

Visual Sound
visualsound.net

WMD Instrument Effects
wmdevices.com

Xotic Pedals
xotic.us

(Zoom) Samson
samsontech.com

EFFECTS INFORMATION RESOURCES

WEBSITES

There are thousands of reviews and videos on the web, or the "disinformation highway" as I like to call it. Gear fanatics who have rarely, if ever, played outside of their bedroom, rec room, or garage, disseminate the vast majority of these. While everyone is entitled to their opinion, some opinions count for more than others. Keep in mind that effects, especially overdrives, often sound only as good as the people playing through them. For the most part, professional players and engineers who have occasion to use these products in context, write the reviews in magazines. Take the reviews and videos with a grain, or better yet, a truckload of salt, and be sure to check out anything that interests you for yourself.

analogman.com

guitargeek.com

kvraudio.com

loopers-delight.com

proguitarshop.com

tonefactor.com

BOOKS

Analog Man's Guide to Vintage Effects. Tom Hughes [For Musicians Only Publishing].

The Boss Book—The Ultimate Guide to the World's Most Popular Compact Effects for Guitar. [Hal Leonard].

Getting Great Guitar Sounds. Michael Ross [Hal Leonard].

Guitar Effects Pedals—The Practical Handbook. Dave Hunter [Backbeat Books].

Sound FX. Alexander U. Case [Focal Press].

Stompbox—A History of Guitar Fuzzes, Flangers, Phasers, Echoes & Wahs. Art Thompson [Miller Freeman Books].

MAGAZINES

Computer Music	*Guitar Player*
Electronic Musician	*Premier Guitar*
EQ	*Sound On Sound*
Future Music	

ABOUT THE AUTHOR

Michael Ross is a musician/writer/producer living in New York City. He has toured the continental United States from California to Cuba playing everything from blues and country to avant-pop and electronica. He is a contributor of reviews, artist features and educational columns to magazines such as *Guitar Player Magazine*, *Premier Guitar*, *Guitar Edge*, *EQ*, *Electronic Musician*, *In Tune*, and *Sound On Sound*— as well as Web sites like Gearwire and Ableton Live. Michael is the author of *Getting Great Guitar Sounds* published by Hal Leonard. He has produced artists in San Francisco and New York.

It is often said of him that he is all about effects.